THE SECOND WORLD WAR

PART 4
The Development of the Great Powers, Denmark and the Netherlands, the Balkan and Danube States, Technological Developments, Submarines, Shipping and Aircraft

Liliane and Fred Funcken

WARD LOCK LIMITED · LONDON

© Illustrations Casterman 1973 and 1974
© Translation Ward Lock 1976

ISBN 0 7063 5081 2

First published in Great Britain 1976 by
Ward Lock Limited, 116 Baker Street,
London, W1M 2BB, a member
of the Pentos Group

Text filmset in Baskerville by
Servis Filmsetting Limited, Manchester

Printed and bound by
Casterman S.A.
Tournai, Belgium

Contents

ARMS and UNIFORMS

Foreword

This is the final volume in the series dealing with the Second World War. Over the years we have been writing these books, our readers have continually told us how much they appreciate this long and arduous task. On many occasions they have anticipated the problems of our work, and have helped us to deal with the more difficult sections. We have also been assisted by eye-witnesses and participants who have sent us vital information which enabled us to correct and complete the details of particular uniforms.

We would like to offer our sincere thanks to the following people for their invaluable help: M. Maurice Chauvet, formerly of the 4th Commando, M. Claude Morin, M. Jacques Lekeu, and once again M. Marcel Boulin, the curator of the Hussar Museum at Tarbes, who so kindly gave us the benefit of his valuable time.

Finally we would like to thank our old friend M. Rene Moulin, Honorary President of the society 'Histoire et Figurines' for all the documentation he so generously put at our disposal.

PART ONE

THE DEVELOPMENT OF THE GREAT POWERS
FRANCE

The Army of Occupied France

After the surrender France was divided into two zones by a line which ran from near Geneva in the east, snaked west to Tours and then continued down to the Spanish border. The Germans occupied the northern half and controlled the French coast as far as the Gulf of Gascony. Vichy, situated on the other side of the line in the 'Free Zone' of non-occupied France, was chosen as the seat of his government by Marshal Philippe Pétain, the last surviving leader of the 1914–18 war and victor of Verdun.

The role of the army was to preserve law and order. It was made up as follows:

Infantry of the Line
18 regiments of 2,240 men, each regiment with 14 Bren guns, 9 grenade launchers, 6 mortars and 4 machine-guns.

Mountain Infantry
6 regiments as above, plus a 700-strong battalion in Corsica.

Cavalry
8 reconnaissance groups of 1,040 men each, with 9 Bren guns, 3 grenade launchers, 2 mortars and 2 machine-guns; 4 mounted regiments with 1,004 men, each with 8 machine-guns and 4 mortars.

Artillery
6 regiments of 1,570 men with some 30 75 mm guns all told; 2 mountain regiments of 1,670 men similarly equipped.

Engineers
8 battalions of engineers, and 8 communications units, some 5,120 men in all.

Mobile Garde Républicaine
3 legions with an effective complement of 6,000 men, 432 Bren guns and 192 machine-guns.

The air force had some 400 fighters, 234 bombers, 26 ground-attack planes, 106 reconnaissance and 90 observation planes in addition to naval aviation, transports and a few squadrons of amphibious torpedo planes. If these figures seem high, it must be remembered that the air force was spread throughout Africa, Indo-China and Syria, with only about 300 planes in France itself. The engine cowlings and tail fins of these planes were painted with wide red and yellow stripes so that they could be easily distinguished by the enemy.

FRANCE, THE MILITIA AND THE RESISTANCE

1. Militia man armed with a captured British Sten Mark 2 9 mm sub-machine-gun. The badge of the province the troops belonged to was often worn on the sleeve. The issue shirt was often replaced by a civilian shirt; contemporary photographs sometimes even show highly unorthodox checked shirts—2. Detail of badge. The gamma symbol of force and rebirth, as well as being the symbol of the ram in astrology, had been chosen as a symbol of the French Militia's revolutionary task

Ranks: 3. Franc-garde—4. Chef de main—5. Chef de dizaine—6. Chef de trentaine adjoint—7. Chef de trentaine—8. Chef de centaine adjoint—9. Chef de centaine—10. Chef de cohorte adjoint—11. Chef de cohorte—12. National flag for Militia—13. Resistance fighter armed with a parachutist's Bren gun of 303 calibre (7.7 mm)—14. Resistance fighter with French 1892 model rifle carrying three 8 mm rounds. He is wearing straw boots for protection in the snow—15. Pendant and arm badges of some of the innumerable Resistance groups

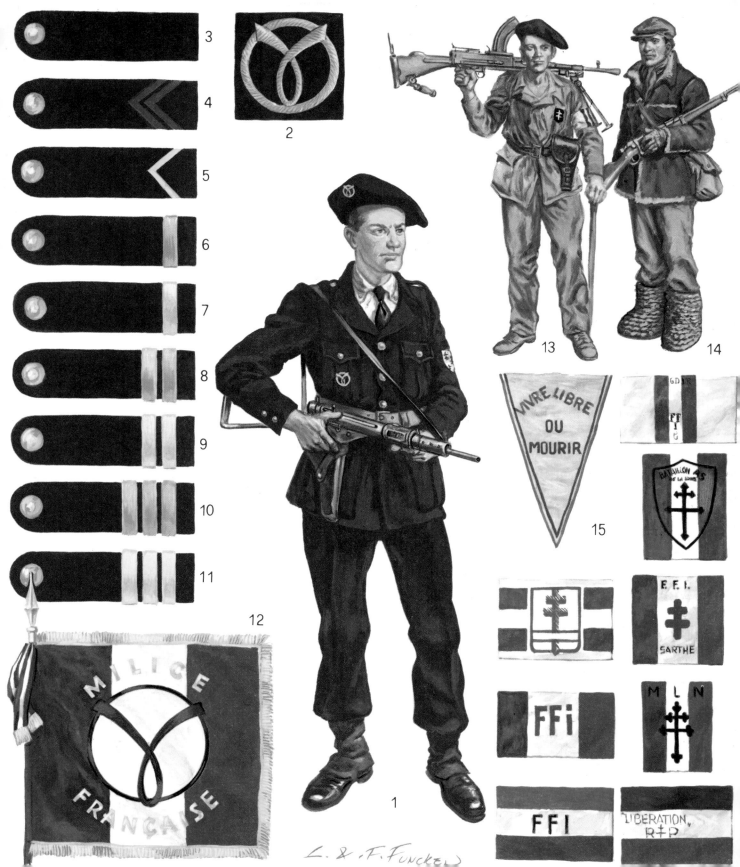

3

4

5

6

7

8

9

10

11

2

12

MILICE

FRANÇAISE

1

13

14

VIVRE LIBRE
OU
MOURIR

15

FFI

FFI

FFi

BATAILLON 4S
DE LA LOIRE

E.F.I.
SARTHE

M L N

LIBERATION
R.T.P.

L. & F. Funcken

French land-based forces were disarmed and disbanded after the Germans invaded the Free Zone in 1942, with the exception of the police force, who were given the job of putting down the Resistance movement, which had been declared illegal by the Vichy government.

The Militia

To preserve law and order Pétain turned the Vichy police force into a Militia, and the Germans soon began to make use of it. This led to a new conflict between the Militia and their compatriots, who were joining the fight in increasing numbers against the puppet government. After a slow start in 1943 the operations and reprisals grew more intense as it became clear that the Germans were losing the war.

In June 1944 the Militia was about 5,000 men strong under the command of ten leaders, and they fought the various Maquis with German help. In general they were armed with Mas 36 rifles, Bren guns (2 to every 10 men) and German sub-machine-guns.

The Maquis in the areas of Corrèze, Jura, Bocage and Brittany – the martyrs of Vercors – obtained their supplies of arms by parachute drops. In 1944 they received some 76,000 Sten guns, 28,000 rifles and carbines, 500 bazookas, 160 mortars, and other supplies of arms by this means.

After the Allied landings and the first signs of the downfall of Germany, the Militia, hated by most of the French and now rejected by Vichy, followed the German retreat and ended their ill-fated life on German soil.

Free French Forces

THE FIRST RALLYING CRY

General de Gaulle's historic appeal from London on 18 June 1940 evoked an immediate response.

FREE FRENCH FORCES AND NEW FRENCH ARMY I

Headgear of soldiers of the 1st Free French Division whose units had joined General de Gaulle before 1 August 1943, after which date they no longer had the right to call themselves Free French. They should not be confused with the French army of Africa, only a few of whose units became a part of the 1st Free French Division. Nonetheless, the 1st Free French Division troops and those of the African army had an equal share in the glory and sacrifice

1. Artillery—2. 13th Engineers—3. Commandant of the 101st Mobile Company, personal field service cap—4. 1st and 2nd Colonial Artillery Regiments, 101st Mobile Company, Division Health Group, 1st West Indian battalion Engineers—5. Army Service Corps—6. 1st North African battalion—7. Health Service—8. Traffic control—9. Communications—10. 13th half-brigade of the Foreign Legion; some sources describe a gold grenade on the right. Surprising as it is to see a beret on the head of a legionnaire, there had been a precedent – a beret similar to that of the Chasseurs Alpins, but of khaki colour, was worn by the same half-brigade during the 1940 landings in Norway—11 and 12. 13th half-brigade of the Foreign Legion—13. 1st Naval Infantry Pacific Battalion. All foot battalion officers wore this field service cap—14. Spahis who had been in Leclerc's division after Tunisia—15. 1st North African Infantry Battalion, 'chèche' for natives—16. 1st Regiment Naval Fusiliers—17. Officer of 1st Regiment Naval Fusiliers—18. English-style helmet of the 1st Free French Division. The same badge was worn on the left sleeve, in a slightly larger version—19. Beret worn by officers of the 1st Tank Squadron, 1st Naval Fusilier Regiment and the 1st Tank Company—20. 'Chéchia' worn by natives in the artillery and foot battalions, nos. 2, 3, 4, 5, 11, 21 and 24.

Field service caps (or berets) of other French Liberation Forces: 21. North African Rifles—22. 3rd Regiment of Moroccan spahis—23. 8th, 16th and 30th Infantry Battalions—24. 12th Cuirassier Regiment, and eventually all other cuirassier regiments—25. Hussars—26. Traffic Police—27. Light Cavalry—28. Hussars—29. Dragoons—30. Dragoons of the 2nd Lancers, formerly the 3rd Black Mountain Corps in the Resistance—31. 1st and 2nd African Rifles—32. 3rd, 5th, 6th, 8th, 9th and 11th African Rifles—33. 2nd spahi Regiment—34. 3rd spahi Regiment—35. 7th spahi Regiment—36. Communications—37. Artillery and Engineers—38. Army Service Corps—39. Zouaves—40. Goum Officers—41. Officers and NCOs in the 4th Moroccan Rifle Regiment—42. Inter-Arms School—43. 46th Infantry Regiment—44. 3rd Algerian spahi Regiment—45. 12th African Riflemen Regiment—46. Moroccan Rifles—47. Airforce—48. Shock Battalions—49. 1st Regiment Parachute Infantry and African Commandos. Other Commando units wore a green beret—50. This black beret was worn by 2nd and 3rd Parachute Regiments until 1944 and by the 501st Tank Regiment—51. SAS (Special Air Service) parachutists and, from 1944, 2nd and 3rd Parachute Regiments

The first to answer the call were those who had escaped from Dunkirk and Norway.

The first Free French navy and air force had hardly been formed when the New Hebrides declared their allegiance to the Resistance on 22 July. Then on 26 and 27 August Chad and the Cameroons followed. On 28 August Brazzaville rose up under the command of the Colonels Delange and Larminat. Once Gabon had been 'liberated' by General Koenig's troops and those of Colonel Parent and Admiral d'Argenlieu, it was not long before the whole of French Equatorial Africa became a part of Free France.

Reinforced by men from lands as far away as Tahiti, New Caledonia and the French bases in India, and inspired by the British, Free France awoke to a new spirit of optimism and national self-respect.

With his forces growing in size, General de Gaulle set up a Council for the defence of the Empire on 27 October. The following month on 18 November the Order of Liberation was founded, and over the next few years this medal was awarded to only 375 men and women, the heroes and heroines of the period.

UNIFORMS

Free French uniforms of the years 1940–4 raise serious difficulties for military historians, because they present a unique and particularly baffling case, especially after the troops' return to Europe.[1]

First it should be remembered that at the time of the surrender in 1940 there were separate French armies in North Africa, Equatorial Africa, Syria, the Lebanon, Somalia, the South Sea Islands and the West Indies.

In 1939 the African army, which was by far the largest, had fifteen infantry divisions and one cavalry division, to say nothing of auxiliaries. Five of these divisions fought in France in May and June 1940 and a sixth was sent to the Middle East. At the time of the surrender there were still ten divisions between Tunis and Morocco. Under the terms of the surrender these forces were again considerably reduced, though demobilisation had already weakened them. This is why, when the Allies landed in North Africa in 1942, there were only five small divisions in Tunisia with uniforms and weapons dating from 1939. This campaign bled the African army white, and left it in need of total reorganisation.

It was then merged with the Egyptian and Chad Free French Forces, who were equipped British-style, and are not to be confused with the African army.

By the time the Lend-Lease programme had rearmed them with American equipment they had been merged with and strengthened by twenty corps of recruits.

Thus in 1944 the Free French army possessed an extraordinary collection of uniforms – the African troops were in Franco-British-American uniforms, Leclerc's famous 2nd Armoured Division had become fairly Americanised, and the troops stationed in the UK were predominantly in British Uniform.

But some regiments kept their complete original French equipment. For example the Moroccan Rifles retained their 1935 helmet and equipment, the greatcoat and plus fours dating from 1938, and a 1916-vintage rifle.[2]

One of the strangest mixtures was in the 2nd Armoured Division, which had American equipment, but one of whose units, a regiment of armoured marine fusiliers or 'saccos', proudly displayed their identity by wearing, according to

2 See Lt-Col P. Carles' excellent study in *La Sabretache*.

FREE FRENCH FORCE AND NEW FRENCH ARMY II

1. Goumier—2. Moroccan rifleman in entirely French uniform—3. Officer in British uniform—4. Moroccan rifleman (landings in Provence)—5. Senegalese rifleman in entirely American uniform—6–8. Officers in mixed Anglo-American uniforms—9–11. Lieutenant, Captain and NCO in the AFAT (Auxiliaires Féminines de L'Armée de Terre) in 1944–1945 (according to the artist well known for his portrayals of the Free French Army, Eugène Lelepfvre) 12. Badge worn on the left arm by officers of the North African Battalion of the 1st Free French Division

1 We would like to thank M. Claude Morin for his valuable help here.

rank, the peaked hat or cap – the 'bachi' – with its red pompom.

Whatever British or American equipment and uniforms they bore, the Free French soldiers of 1944 always kept their own caps, if necessary adapting foreign ones, and kept their traditional gold and silver braiding.

Take for example some little-known troops from far away: the Pacific battalion stationed on Tahiti. They were dressed in navy blue with khaki caps and naval gaiters, while the troops defending Saint-Pierre-et-Miquelon wore British uniforms and French caps.

We will discuss the Commandos and their special clothing in the section on volunteer forces in Great Britain.

The Goums or Arab contingents who took part in some of the hardest fighting of the Liberation looked particularly exotic and fierce. Founded as an auxiliary corps in 1908 the Goums (literally 'troops' in Arabic) acted as infantry, cavalry and mule-train rolled into one. The command structure had a French captain at the top, three French or Algerian lieutenants, and French or Algerian NCOs and other ranks. A curious system of numbering was in operation by 1939. Each active Goum, numbered from 1–57, could be reinforced by raising its own auxiliaries, and these would add 100 or 200 to their parent number, so that the 29th Goum, for instance, had the 129th Goum as first auxiliary and the 229th as second.

In 1942 the 102 Goums in existence were grouped into tabars or battalions of three plus one command Goum. They fought superbly under General Guillaume, principally in Italy and France. Their uniform was a mixture of Arabic and European styles.

The headdress or 'khiout': made of plaits of wool knotted together in the colour of the group.

The coat or 'djellaba': a long coat with a hood, with white, grey and black, or brown and black stripes, or mottled.

The 'gandourah': a long sleeveless blouse.

The 'serouat': very full trousers worn by the Moroccan Spahis and Zouaves, sometimes replaced by narrower calf-length trousers.

The full jacket: replaced by a jacket or khaki windcheater.

'Tarouines': a kind of woollen stocking without feet, tightly or loosely knit.

'Naïls': Arab sandals.

'Chkara': a kind of leather haversack.

One of the most famous units, the 4th Moroccan mountain division or *DeMeMe* was nicknamed the 'Royal Brêls' after the British had borrowed their mules (in Arabic 'brêl') to climb the narrow path along the River Garigliano, which flows south of Monte Cassino.

FOREIGN VOLUNTEERS IN GREAT BRITAIN

1 and 2. 1st Battalion Navy Commandos Fusiliers from July 1941 to the end of 1942. The Cross of Lorraine worn with the beret was replaced in June 1943 by the badge shown in fig. 3—3. French No. 4 commando in uniform worn for the 1944 landing—4. Polish forces in Libya (1941–42)—5. Infantryman of Polish corps in Great Britain—6. A Polish Volunteer Tank Lieutenant. On the left sleeve one can see the 2nd armoured division badge; on the right sleeve, the insignia of the British 8th Army commemorating the victory at Cassino (fig. 17)

7–11. Shoulder flashes. 'FF Commando' stands for 'Free French Commando'—12. Badge worn by all British Commandos including foreign volunteers—13. Badge, fig. 1—Arm badges: 14. Belgian forces before September 1944—15. Dutch—16. 2nd Polish Division—17. British 8th Army at Cassino—18. Czechoslovak—19. Belgian Armoured Cars Squadron beret badge—20. Belgian after September 1944

21. The Commando memorial erected at Spean Bridge near Inverlochy, Scotland, in 1952 to the memory of commandos of all nationalities killed during the Second World War, for this was the area where they trained

14

15

16

17

18

19

20

7 POLAND

8 FRANCE

9 N°4 COMMANDO

10 F.F. COMMANDO

11 4 COMMANDO

12

13

21 UNITED WE CONQUER

1 2 3 4 5 6

GREAT BRITAIN

Foreign Volunteers

A law was passed on 31 August 1940 which enabled France, Belgium, Holland, Czechoslovakia, Poland and Norway to recruit volunteers to be equipped and trained in Britain, from among their refugees who had fled to Britain.

At first glance most of these foreign volunteers looked British. The only concession made to their nationality was a narrow stripe sewn high on the sleeve and following the curve of the shoulder, which bore their country's name in white written in English.

Some contingents, for example, the French and the Polish, even managed to preserve their way of showing the wearer's rank. Since it would have been out of place to wear a British regiment's insignia, they wore their own cap badges.

So each country adopted one or more national or regimental insignia. For example, the Belgians who made up the Belgian Armoured Cars Squadron, under the 1st Derbyshire Yeomanry wore British battledress and the tank corps' black beret, but with the addition of a silver Belgian lion.

This beret, the only one worn in the British army at that time, dates back longer than is generally thought, and has a curious history. In 1917 some Royal Tank Corps officers decided to keep up the old British military tradition of adopting the enemy's headgear after each war. But a twist of fate had them adopt instead the beret of their valiant ally, France. A unit of Chasseurs Alpins was billeted nearby and their enormous alpine berets were much admired. They were considered to be a trifle too large, however, and while they were looking for a smaller model, someone suggested writing to British girls' schools for samples. The response was magnificent, and from the vast selection, a black prototype was chosen. It was of course quite another thing to have it accepted by the War

Office, but it was finally approved in 1925.

The original national uniforms, which officers had been allowed to wear off duty, gradually disappeared, although just before D-Day hosts of special badges began to appear, some of which we have illustrated.

FOREIGN VOLUNTEERS IN THE RAF AND ROYAL NAVY

We have already mentioned the distinguished role played by foreign flyers in the RAF. Naturally the French were the largest contingent, providing at least ten out of the hundred or so fighter squadrons and nearly as many bomber squadrons.

Each group had its own emblem taken from the coat of arms of a province, such as Lorraine, Guyenne, Normandy, Artois, Alsace, etc. To a greater extent than other foreign volunteers the French tended to keep their own uniforms, sometimes combining them with those of the RAF, and wearing them in this way both on and off duty.

The Fighting or Free French Navy was reinforced by young men who had escaped from France or its overseas territories and in 1943 numbered some 50 ships including many destroyers and more than 6,000 men. In the highest tradition of the French navy, vessels such as the submarines *Narval* and *Surcouf* and the frigate *Mimosa* were lost while on active service.

BRITISH ARMY, PARATROOPERS AND COMMANDOS

1 and 2. Parachute officer and soldier in service dress—3. Sergeant in the Glider Pilots Regiment, most of whose numbers were killed in crashes before the landings in Normandy—4. Parachutist in battle dress with folding motor cycle dropped by container—5. Parachutist in battle dress with Sten Mark V sub-machine-gun—6. Commando with a PIAT gun (Projector Infantry Anti-Tank). Detail of loading—7. Commando with Lee Enfield No. 4 Mark I rifle—8. Commando with Thompson sub-machine-gun—9. Commando with K-gun and magazines—10. Special Commando dagger. British Commandos wore their original regiment's badge on their beret

THE PARATROOPS

We should begin with the 1st Airborne Infantry Company or 1st Free French Parachute Company under Captain Berge, who retained his full 1940 infantry officer's uniform. His men, however, wore British uniform but with the khaki French forage cap. They belonged to the Special Air Service or SAS, and this 1st Company, founded in 1940, was to become in 1943 the 3rd Battalion SAS and in 1944 the Light Infantry Parachute Regiment. They became known as the 'Sky Battalion' and were dropped over Brittany on the night of 5 and the morning of 6 June 1944.

A fourth SAS battalion set up in 1943 became the 3rd Light Infantry Parachute Regiment in 1944 and was then merged with the 2nd Regiment in 1945. Finally, a regiment set up in North Africa in 1943 became the 1st Regiment.

During the years which preceded the D-Day landings, the French paratroopers adopted first the forage cap of the air force, and then the black beret. The SAS sent to North Africa were issued with a sand-coloured beret, while their British counterparts already wore the famous red beret.

On their return to Great Britain, the French paratroopers were eager to retain their beige beret which distinguished them from the other troops. Standardisation only came about in 1944, when King George VI granted the French paratroopers the right to wear the red beret, in recognition of their services. For once they were all dressed in the same uniform when they marched for the first time along the Champs-Elysées on 11 November 1944.

The uniform was identical to that of the British, and was very similar to the battledress of the infantry, except in the style of the trousers. The insignia of the paratroopers consisted of two outspread wings with a parachute in the centre, which was issued after the first mission and worn on the sleeve. After the third mission it was worn on the breast. An almost identical insignia, but more elaborately decorated, was fastened on the beret. The British Imperial crown over the insignia did not appear on the French beret.

THE COMMANDOS

The origins of the Commandos will be described further on. Here too there was a similarly slow but steady movement towards the anglicisation of uniforms while – more noticeably here than in the parachute regiments – some elements of their original uniforms survived.

Without doubt the most noticeable example was the famous 1st Battalion of Naval Fusilier Commandos who, until the end of 1942, wore caps and bachis with red pompoms together with their battledress. It was only at the end of 1942 or the beginning of 1943 that Lieutenant Philippe Kieffer's men began to wear the famous green beret. Until then, even at the time of the bloody Dieppe raid in 1942, French Commandos, who were the first French soldiers to fight on their native soil since the surrender, wore caps decorated with gold anchors or hats with red pompoms.

The 177 brave men of the Kieffer Commando unit, whose chief became a Major and was later to land in France on D-Day, chose as their last badge the model of June 1943. This was a bronze shield with a little cross of Lorraine in the upper left, a ship in the middle crossed by a Commando dagger, and under it a scroll reading 'Commandos Marines'. Apart from the shoulder stripe and the beret badge, the uniform was completely British even if the webbing equipment was nicknamed 'brêlage' (no doubt a reference to the packs carried by Arab mules).[1]

1 See the chapter on the Free French Forces: the Goums. The word 'brêlage' originally referred to something held together with ropes, but the Arab word 'brêl' (mule) may have given the expression a new lease of life.

BRITISH ARMY, VARIOUS UNIFORMS

1. Infantryman in FSMO (Field Service Marching Order)— 2. MP (Military Police) wearing cap—3. MP in helmet (Europe 1945)—4. Officer—5. Sapper with Special Unit in new model helmet and multiple pocket canvas waistcoat— 6. Gurkha with traditional weapon, the frightful *kukriss*— 7 and 8. Officer and soldier fighting in Malaya. They are wearing the slouch hat borrowed from the Boers during the Boer War—9. Sapper with special waistcoat as shown in fig. 5. On his arm he wears the special badge worn on the landing beaches—10 and 11. Infantrymen. Fig. 10 wears special lightweight landing equipment—12. Tank Officer

Besides these British Commandos we should mention the French and African Commandos and shock troops. For all of these the principal badge worn on the left sleeve was a red star with the cross of Lorraine. A dark blue beret was worn. As well as this, French Commandos wore the flanged 1940 tank helmet.

The British

The preceding text and illustrations show how few and far between were the modifications made to the general appearance of the British army's uniforms. Some special units' coloured berets and the badges of certain larger corps (which combined symbolic, historical and mythical symbols dear to a people well acquainted with the past) alone broke the monotony of khaki.

Sometimes the narrow rectangle of a 'flash' gave a touch of colour – red for infantry, yellow and red for cavalry, red and blue for artillery, yellow and green for reconnaissance units.

There were few exceptions, but one of the most characteristic was the Tank Corps' adoption of beige or brown corduroy trousers, although it should be noted that in this case the example had been set in typical British style by the man who beat Rommel, Bernard Law, Lord Montgomery of Alamein. The regulation-issue, buttoned battle-dress was even uglier than the model with concealed buttons, and was made at the end of the war.

The only new items in the British soldiers' wardrobe were the Canadian sleeveless leather jerkin, the many-pocketed pioneer jacket and a new helmet that was issued only on a small scale.

PARATROOPS AND COMMANDOS

Set up in 1940, the British paratroops were used for the first time on a large scale in Sicily. They took part in the Normandy landings on 6 June 1944 and then in Provence and Nimègue where they suffered enormous losses.

The Commandos were set up in June 1940,

largely on Winston Churchill's initiative, by Lt-Colonel Dudley Clarke. It was he rather than Churchill who suggested the name Commando – a name of Portuguese origin which the Boers in South Africa had used originally for their expeditions against the Zulus. At first, Combined Operations Command recruited volunteers only from the army, but from 1942 it recruited from the Royal Marines as well. It should be noted that British Commandos kept their own regiment's badges on their green berets. The famous No. 4 Commando comprised a small group of volunteers from Luxembourg, as well as French Naval Fusiliers. The illustrations and the section on volunteers describe their uniform. Commando operations were among the most spectacular. In 1941 at Lofoten, at Spitsbergen and in Norway, in 1942 at Saint-Nazaire and Dieppe and finally in 1944 in Normandy, all were splendid examples of selfless courage.

Special Armoured Vehicles

The catastrophic raid on Dieppe on 19 August 1942 revealed a major problem in the many kinds of anti-invasion techniques that the enemy used. Dieppe had cost the 2nd Canadian Division 3,369 killed, wounded or captured out of a total of 5,000 men to say nothing of the Commandos' losses.

SPECIAL ARMOURED VEHICLES

1. Sherman DD (Duplex Drive), nicknamed 'Donald Duck'. Devised as a surprise tactic, it was more of a mortal trap for the heroes of the 79th Brigade on D-Day—2. Churchill with a 290 mm gun that fired a 36 lb hollow-charge round, nicknamed 'Flying Dustbin'—3. Sherman with 'Lulu Detector'—4. Churchill 'Twaby Ark' bridge-layer—5. Churchill bridge-layer—6. Churchill 'Carpet-layer', for unstable ground or areas where there were heavy barbed-wire entanglements. To the rear and on the sides can be seen the arrangement enabling the motors to 'breathe', so that the tank could move in water 6 ft deep

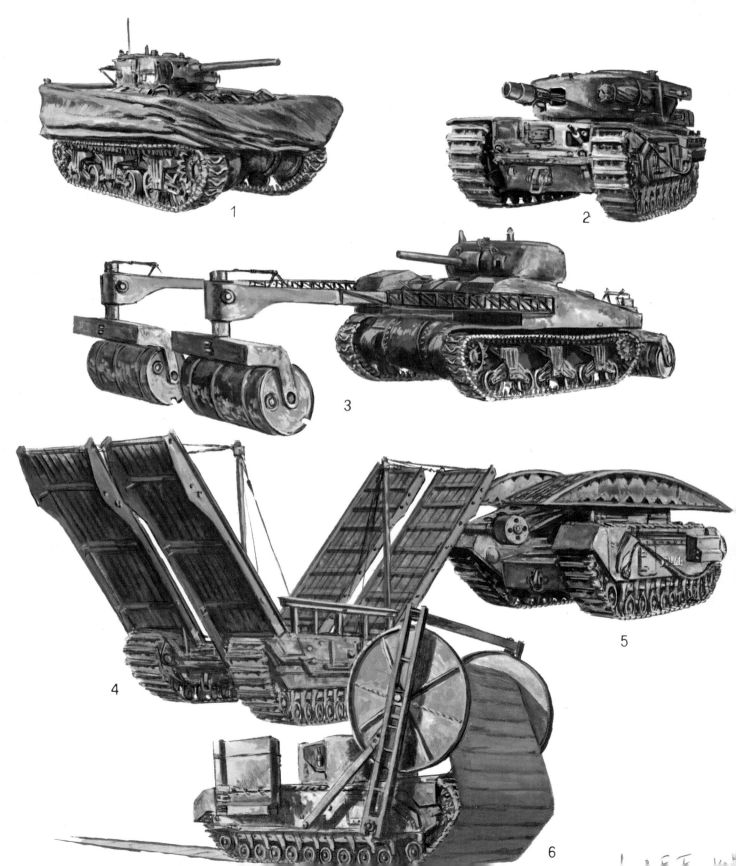

1

2

3

4

5

6

The extraordinary flail tanks or 'Scorpions' of the famous 'Scorpion Regiment' first appeared in North Africa and had been created by a retired general officer who was at the time a corporal in the Home Guard, Major-General Sir Percy Hobart, 'Hobo' to his men. He was responsible for developing the 79th Armoured Division's special tanks that were essential to the D-Day success. Thanks to this retired officer's ceaseless toil, an astonishingly wide range of perfectly adapted vehicles saw the light of day.

Between 1943 and the end of the war in Europe the 79th Armoured Division gradually became the largest British unit, with more than 1,500 special tanks which were divided up as follows:
One brigade of Canal Defence Light (CDL) searchlight tanks
One brigade of 'Crocodiles' – Churchill tanks equipped with flamethrowers
One brigade of 'Avres' – 'Armoured Vehicles Royal Engineers'
Five British regiments of amphibious Duplex Drive (DD) tanks
Two Canadian regiments of Duplex Drive (DD) tanks
Three American battalions of Duplex Drive (DD) tanks
Two Anglo-Canadian regiments of armoured 'Kangaroo' troop transporters
Six regiments of American Landing Vehicles Tracked (LVT) amphibious tanks or 'Buffalos'

The 'Avres' brigade had the strangest vehicles, such as the flail tank whose chains whipped the ground ahead to detonate any mines and which existed in various guises under the names of 'Marquis', 'Crab', 'Scorpion', 'Lulu' or 'Cird' (Canadian Indestructible Roller Device).

Then there were the ingenious bridge-layers and other vehicles designed to get over all kinds of obstacles. The strange appearance of these machines – they were nicknamed 'Funnies' – should not make one forget the 460 men of this special corps who were killed.

Though the British usually claim that the DD tank was meant as a tactical surprise, this amphi-bious version of the 30 ton Sherman tank was a tragic failure when tried out on 6 June. Of the thirty DDs launched into rough waters, only five arrived on the beach, and three of those thanks only to the bravery of the LCT[1] skippers who launched them almost onto the beach, having witnessed with horror the drowning of 135 crew of the 79th Brigade.

The Americans preferred to use genuine am-phibious tanks like the LVT 'Buffalo' mentioned above, armed with two 20 mm guns or a single 75 mm howitzer.

An American sergeant named Cullin invented some wire-clippers which could be readily put together from the debris of anti-tank barriers. These made possible the famous breakthrough into Saint-Lô when they destroyed the natural obstacle provided by the tangled hedgerows of the Normandy Bocage.

1 See below Landing Craft in the chapter on the American navy.

BRITISH AVIATION

1. Commonwealth CA 12 Boomerang. Although only 250 were constructed in great haste, this squat, rugged little fighter enabled the Royal Australian air force to hold off the first Japanese attacks, while they waited for massive reinforce-ments of Spitfires and Kittyhawks. They fought in the skies above the Solomons, Borneo and New Guinea—2. Hawker Typhoon, the best ground-attack fighter—3. Gloster Meteor, the first Allied jet fighter—4. Westland Whirlwind; although this long-range fighter was a great morale booster for the populations of occupied countries, it suffered from numerous faults. 112 examples were built for the RAF, the last Whirl-wind coming out of the factory in January 1942—5. De Havilland Mosquito, one of the most remarkable planes of the Second World War. The FB VI was the most common (1943)—6. Hawker Tempest. The final development of the Typhoon, it was superior in performance. It destroyed more than 600 V1s in 3 months and was the fighter best able to take on the Me-262, of which it destroyed at least 20—7. Insignia painted on dark fuselages from 1942–1945—8. Insignia painted on light fuselages – grey and green camouflage appeared in 1942. The 3-coloured flash on the tail with a narrow white central stripe was standardised in July 1942

The Royal Air Force

The British White Paper of November 1944 on the war effort mentions that between January and June of that year 2,889 heavy bombers, 1,391 light bombers and 5,655 fighter planes were built. Taking into account all planes constructed, including those for flying schools, naval aviation, air transport, air-sea rescue and reconnaissance, we get a total of 102,609 planes. It may seem astonishing that in comparison with this enormous figure only 3,000 to 4,000 planes were ready for front-line combat duties, but one should not forget that, for example, in 1943 four out of six planes that came out of the factory had to return for major repairs. Disregarding the possibility of its being destroyed in action or by accident, a plane lasted for only eight or nine months of active service.

Some of the great aircraft mentioned in the preceding volume of this series went through a number of developments. The Spitfire, for example, went from a Mk V to a Mk XIX. The Mk XIV Spitfire of 401 squadron was the first to shoot down a Messerschmitt Me-262, and was to be the most successful plane against the V1 flying bombs. The ground attack version of the Hurricane was less successful; weighed down by four 60 lb rocket bombs, it could only manage some 200 mph, and this made it an easy target for German anti-aircraft guns defending the flying-bomb launch-ramps.

Another member of the Hawker family, the Typhoon, was far more efficient and played a large part in the success of the landings and the Allied breakthrough to the Rhine. In a single day in August 1944 Typhoons alone destroyed 135 enemy tanks. Raymond Lallemant, the Belgian ace, destroyed 34 tanks while flying a Typhoon. The last Hawker plane of the war, the Tempest, first appeared in January 1944, and was the most powerful single-engined plane in the RAF. It was particularly effective against the V1, of which it destroyed 638 in four months. Specially detailed to Messerschmitt Me-262 interception, Tempests managed to destroy twenty, a considerable achievement. Pierre Clostermann, the great French ace, pulled off the crowning successes of his extraordinary life at the controls of a Tempest.[1]

The first and only Allied jet plane, the Gloster Meteor, first saw battle in June 1944. The first jets flew against V1s before being sent to fight in Europe. When they arrived in Holland in April 1945 these fine British jet planes never had the chance to challenge their German equivalents; of the 280 Meteors built, few saw service before the war was over.

1 33 fighters, 24 bombers, 72 locomotives, 25 trucks, 5 tanks, 2 high-speed launches and (jointly) 1 submarine.

SOVIET ARMY I

New uniform. Field service dress
1. Soldier of the Guard. Above the right pocket he wears a special badge, shown in detail on either side. Small chevrons indicate a severe wound (gold) and a light wound (red). Under the same pocket one can see the badge of excellence, shown in greater detail between figs 2 and 3. On the left the soldier has the gold star given together with the Order of Lenin, making him a 'Hero of the Soviet Union'—2. Soldier of the Guard Unit with severe wound chevron (see above). On the left he is wearing ribbons of medals given for bravery and good conduct in war—3. Telephonist Pioneer—4. Officer with ribbon of Order of the Red Star (14th most important Russian medal)—5. Officer with hooded cape. He wears a plaque of the Order of the Red Star (shown on his right)—6. One-piece camouflage outfit—7 and 8. Infantryman with full equipment—9. Cossack—10. Infantryman seen from back—11. Woman soldier in Army Service Corps (the letter P on her arm-badge corresponds to R in the Russian alphabet, for Ruler). Soviet women took a considerable part in the fighting, even in armoured divisions

The Red Army

In spite of the non-aggression pact signed by the two nations, the Soviet Union was ready to fight the Reich on the eve of the German invasion.

The invasion of Poland in September 1939 led to general mobilisation under which, thanks to a new law, 'all male Soviet citizens of whatever race, creed, social origin, education or position' were called up.

Some years previously the age requirement had dropped from 21 to 19, and before then future conscripts had to undergo three years of preparatory training. Workers and students learned how to handle infantry weapons and tactics on a company level, and had to spend two weeks in camp on manoeuvres.

Military service lasted two years and was divided into two distinct parts. The first was spent on the infantryman's basic physical training, weapon handling and combat tactics. Conscripts received elementary lessons in administration, health and veterinary care as well, of course, as a political education the importance of which we have already established in the first volume of this series.

When this first stage of training was complete, the conscript swore an oath of allegiance and began the training that would make him a *krasnoarmeyets* or 'man of the Red Army'.[1] Exercises continued as before with additional manoeuvres in squads and machine-gun and mortar practice. This was followed by battle training, in conjunction with the artillery and engineer corps.

If in the course of these two years the recruit had not obtained promotion, he was returned to civilian life. If he had become a non-commissioned officer, he would follow another year in the appropriate course. For the next three years soldiers would have refresher courses at periodic intervals, staying in the 1st reserves up to the age of 35, in the 2nd up to the age of 45 and in the 3rd to 50.

As we showed in the first volume of this series, not all young men went into the armed forces, since the larger proportion of Soviet citizens was drafted into territorial units whose functions we have explained.

Students were allowed to complete their studies before entering the army as candidate officers or non-commissioned officers.

From 1939 the territorial units were made part of the regular army once more. The youngest territorials, who were part of the emergency reserve, could be called up in a few hours. If the second reserves were needed they could reinforce the first on a large scale, transforming companies into battalions, battalions into regiments and regiments into divisions. The third reserves acted as powerful reinforcements and could be armed, trained and ready for action in three months. The

SOVIET ARMY II

1. Colonel in short fur coat called the *Shubavalenki*. It came in various colours from off-white to beige. It was made from sheepskin worn fur side inside. Crack troops also wore it. Fur boots with leather trim were generally reserved for officers—2. Nurse—3. Artillery Officer—4. Artillery Lieutenant—5. One-piece hooded camouflage uniform. There was also a jacket in the same style—6. *Shturmanka* tunic and padded trousers, also worn with broadcloth trousers—7. Snow jacket and matching trousers—8. Soldier in the workers' militia (conscripted for the defence of Moscow, their relative inexperience led to heavy losses). Note size of 1910 Maxim machine-gun partially covered and painted white—9. Molotov cocktail with fuse and instructions on label—10. Telephonist. Communications soldiers wore an epaulette showing the arm they were attached to, but only in the echelon of the battalion or regiment—11. Nurse. Women in auxiliary services did not hesitate to take arms—12. Infantryman in greatcoat wearing under his helmet the old pointed *budionovka*, also known as the *shlem*

---

1 On 3 October 1946 the name 'Red Army' was replaced by 'Soviet Army'. The Red soldier was, as a consequence, called a *ryadovoy* or man of the ranks.

fourth and last reserves were sent to different reception areas to be ready to perform as last-ditch reinforcements.

At the critical moment this system, which had been devised so carefully, functioned perfectly. Without it the USSR would have been completely annihilated.

During the war the minimum age for recruitment dropped to 18 for most conscripts and to 17 for secondary-school pupils. Ordinary soldiers were sent to the front after four to twelve months' training, depending on the arm of service with which they would fight.

Various military schools provided the huge Red Army with its officers. In 1918 Frunze, the People's Commissar, founded the most famous of these, the Frunze Academy. From this academy came all those great generals who were to win world-wide fame during this war, in a confrontation which was to cost the lives of 7,500,000 Russian soldiers, that is, one out of every 22 of the population of the USSR in 1940. These men sometimes came from the most humble backgrounds and, unlike the officers of the Tsar's army, were of many creeds and races. Men like Zhukov, the one-time sergeant; Vatutin, a peasant; Chernyakovsky, a Jew; and Bagramian, an Armenian, all showed extraordinary intelligence and bravery, and finally put paid to the myth of German invincibility.

THE NEW UNIFORM

On 6 January 1943 the President of the Supreme Soviet issued a decree to replace the badges of rank worn on the collar and sleeves with epaulettes which were almost identical to those of the old Tsarist army. This action restored the old military traditions of the Russian people, rising above their hatred of the régime that the Revolution had abolished. Together with these *pogony*, the system of saluting officers was brought back, and their privileges continued to increase. Pay also increased considerably with rank: a marshal of the Soviet Union was paid 114 times as much as an ordinary soldier.

NKVD TROOPS

After the Revolution, the Russian Communist party had been forced to create an organisation to fight internal political opposition. This is the origin of the *Cheka* or 'Chrezvychainaya Kommissia' (Extraordinary Commission), which was to become better known in the West under its new name of GPU from 1922, and later the NKVD[1] in 1934.

There were some 300,000 men in the NKVD troops, almost up to division strength, who fought beside the regular Red Army divisions on the front. They fought well but were never a special or élite division.

DISCIPLINARY BATTALIONS

Discipline was strict and violations of duty were severely punished. In peace time insubordination meant military service for from two months to two years. In wartime insulting the nation in this way received three to seven years' imprisonment or transfer to those disciplinary battalions who undertook the most dangerous missions. There men who had been absent without leave rubbed shoulders with criminals of all kinds, including those who had been condemned to death and had been offered a way of buying back their lives.

1 *Narodnyi Komissariat Vnoutrennikh Diel* – The People's Commissariat for Internal Affairs.

SOVIET ARMY III

Ranks: 1. Marshal of the Soviet Union—2. Marshal (head of a particular arm, here Engineers)—3. Artillery Marshal—4. General—5. Colonel-General—6. Lieutenant-General (air force)—7. Major-General—8. Ditto (Veterinary service)—9. Epaulette for Marshal of the Soviet Union in field service dress. Figs. 2–8 follow this principle, substituting dark green for gold background. Figs. 10–17 show epaulettes of service dress and field service dress—10. Infantry Colonel—11. Artillery Lt-Colonel—12. Commissariat Major—13. Administrative Services Major—14. Flight-Lieutenant—15. 1st Lieutenant Infantry—16. Tank Lieutenant—17. 2nd Lieutenant, Cavalry

18. Marshals' and Generals' button—19. Officers', NCOs' and Soldiers' button—20. General Officer in working dress—21. Superior Officer of Guard Artillery in service dress. He has been decorated twice with the title 'Hero of the Soviet Union'

1 2 3 4 5 6 7

9 10 11 12 13

14 15

16 17

20 18 19 21

At first NKVD officers were put in charge of these oddly mixed companies, but so many were murdered that officers had to be chosen from among the convicts themselves. In this way, order was preserved.

Many were the acts of bravery and self-sacrifice performed by these disciplinary battalions. These actions were prompted by the hope that if a man were wounded heroically enough he might be pardoned, and even get back his citizen's rights together with the pay and privileges of a regular soldier in the Red Army.

SIBERIAN TROOPS

Though often described as Asiatic soldiers, the Siberian élite divisions were, on the contrary, made up of a large proportion of European Russians, including woodsmen, miners, workmen and agricultural labourers who had emigrated to this huge territory in ever-increasing numbers from the seventeenth century onwards. Then came the Kazakhs – a mixed half-European half-Mongol race and finally the Yakuts and the pure Mongol – Buryats – whose total population was less than 3,000,000. It was only during the thirties that the 12,000,000 Chukchis, an Eskimo race, were 'Sovietised'. They provided no conscripts.

THE SNIPERS

Like the Germans and the Japanese, the Russians used snipers on a wide scale, but were the first to use women in this form of combat; Pavluchenko, one of the most famous, distinguished herself during the siege of Sebastopol.

THE SAPPERS

Of all the countries fighting Germany, Russia was the first to learn just how powerful were the Wehrmacht's counter-attacks. So they devised a way of holding on to land gained at considerable expense: before attacking a position, the Russians would send sappers with the assault troops to lay minefields according to a carefully prepared plan.

When the Germans were pushed back, the sappers followed them, mining the ground behind them. Some special groups dug themselves in and waited for the counter-attack, laying traps in the way of the armoured vehicles' line of retreat, while the tanks were still attacking. One can easily imagine what an extremely tricky job it was to carry this out while the battle raged.

Light Arms

WINTER GREASE

The story has often been told of how the cold jammed the German light arms, while Soviet arms were not affected, ostensibly because the latter were constructed to such wide tolerances that ice made no difference. However, the laws of ballistics and the way in which guns work discount this explanation. In fact the mystery was simply a matter of a special grease that the Russians had perfected long ago.

SOVIET ARMY IV

1. Artillery Starchina (Company Sergeant-Major) — 2. Pioneers 1st Sergeant-Major—3. Armoured Corps Sergeant-Major—4. Military Administration Sergeant attached to the Cavalry—5. Infantry Corporal—6. Cavalry Soldier—7. Infantry Soldier. The second row shows epaulettes worn with field service dress

Command Schools: 8. Artillery—9. Communications—10. Infantry—11. Cavalry—*Services:* 12. Commissariat—13. Veterinary—*Technical Schools:* 14. Artillery—15. Communications—*Cadet field service dress epaulettes:* 16. Artillery—17. Infantry—18. Cavalry

Badge insignia: 19. Infantry (worn by NKVD Infantry only)—20. Cavalry (some claim it was silver)—21. Engineers—22. Road Maintenance Troops—23. Pioneers—24. Pontoneers—25. Artillery—26. Surveyors—27. Military railways—28. Communications — 29. Military Justice — 30. Rocket-launchers and mortars—31. Commissariat—32. Music—33. Chemical warfare—34. Medical Corps—35. Mobilised Troops—36. Veterinary—37. Tanks

38. Old-style field service cap with double row of piping in the colour of the service—39. Plain field service cap worn from 1943–1945. The red star was replaced in combat by a dark green one—40. Student at Cavalry Officers' Training School in service dress

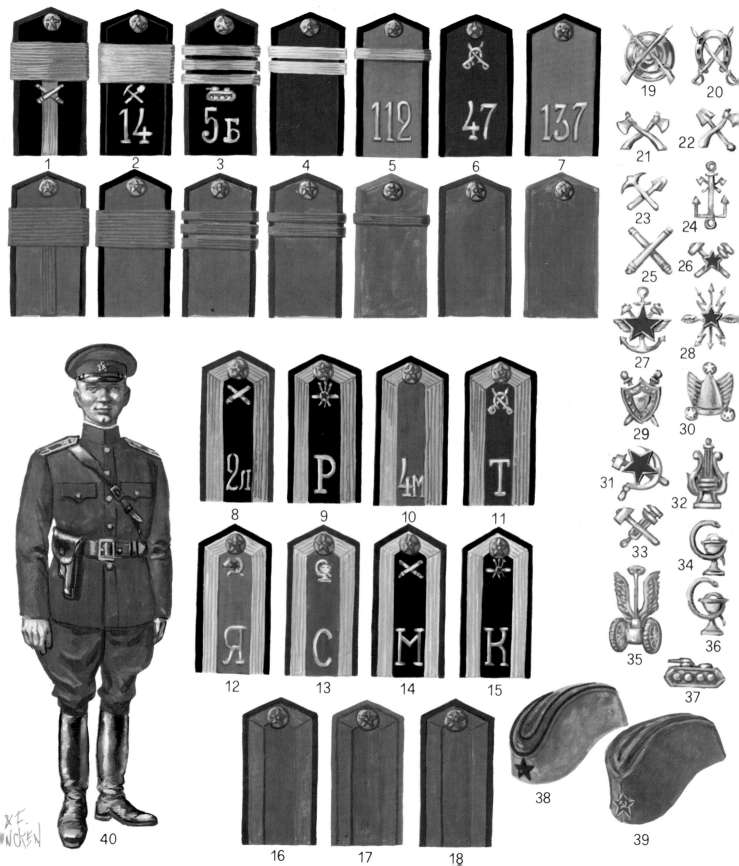

1
2
3
4
5
6
7

14
5Б
112
47
137

19
20
21
22
23
24
25
26
27
28
29
30
31
32
33
34
35
36
37

8
9
10
11

2Л
Р
4М
Т

12
13
14
15

Я
С
М
К

16
17
18

38
39
40

RIFLES

The Soviet rifleman's traditional weapon, the 1891/30 model rifle, stayed in use throughout the war and was not replaced by the completely new Tokarev semi-automatic rifle, which appeared around 1943. The Tokarev, which fired 20–30 rounds a minute, proved too complicated from the start. It required long and painstaking maintenance and had a tiresome tendency to misfire.

The 1944 model carbine was the only new model based on a traditional weapon, and its performance and silhouette were exactly the same as those of the 1938 model carbine, which we showed in volume 1 of this series. The only small differences were a slightly longer barrel and an unsheathed bayonet, which was fixed 'at ease' along the barrel.

SUB-MACHINE-GUNS

The Soviet army was the first to equip its infantry with machine pistols, doing so immediately after the first Russo-Finnish war. The Finns used a Suomi 9 mm sub-machine-gun which, according to some observers, caused 70% of Russian losses.

When the Germans attacked, Red Army riflemen had been issued with large numbers of sub-machine-guns of two different kinds, the Degtiarev PPD 1940, and the Shpagin 1941, the latter being distinguished particularly by its curved magazine. The Degtiarev fired between 900 and 1,100 rounds a minute and the Shpagin between 700 and 900 rounds. Mass production of the PPD was soon found to be too slow and too expensive, because of its relative complexity; besides, its rival, the Shpagin, was highly thought of by the troops, who knew best.

Meanwhile Sudayev, a Soviet engineer, had managed to perfect a completely new model, the PPS 43, with a folding metal butt. Lighter, easier to handle and far simpler to construct and maintain, this weapon, which had the same 7.62 mm calibre as its rivals, had a slower rate of fire: 650 rounds a minute. It could be used to fire short bursts or single shots, and this considerably reduced the amount of ammunition it used, which until then had been prohibitive, while at the same time subjecting the barrel and firing mechanism to less wear.

More and more machine-pistols were issued, so that by the end of the war they had increased 21-fold. It goes without saying that this profusion gave the Red Infantry far more fire-power than any other allied or enemy army and played an important role in Russian offensive combat.

MACHINE-GUNS

The old 1910 model Maxim continued its work valiantly despite the appearance of its replacement, the DS 1939, which had very disappointing results and was quickly replaced by the D.Sh.K.

SOVIET ARMY V

1 and 2. Peaked hat and *papacha* of Marshal and General. Above, detail of badge—Headgear of other ranks down to ordinary soldier: 3. Cavalry—4. Colonel's *papacha*—5. Artillery—6. Detail of badge.

NKVD troops: 7. Lieutenant-General—8. Artillery Lieutenant-Colonel—9. Major in the Commissariat—10. 2nd Lieutenant in the Militia—11. Starchina (Regimental Sergeant-Major)—12. Sergeant-Major (Technician)—13. Convoy Escort, 1st Sergeant-Major—14. Convoy Escort, Sergeant—15. NKVD cap—Collar patches for coats: 16. Officer in Internal Security Service—17. Soldier—18. Convoy Escort cap. Below: Cap worn by *Obergruppe* of the NKVD

Frontier guards (a separate entity in the Soviet Army, they were part of the Home Guard with the NKVD): 19. Major-General—20. Major—21. Captain—22. Lieutenant (Technician)—23. 1st Lieutenant (abroad)—24. Sergeant—25. Corporal—26. Soldier—27. Frontier Guard's cap—28. Lapel patch for Generals' coats—29. Lapel patch for officers' and troops' coats—30. Frontier Guard Officer in field service dress with variation on cap. From a total of 150,000 men before the war, the Frontier Guard Service had grown to 400,000 in 1950

Lapel patches from ground army coats, Marshals and Generals: 31. Infantry and Cavalry—32. Artillery and Armoured Corps—33. Engineers and Technical Services—34. Medical and Veterinary Services—Officers, NCOs and soldiers: 35. Cavalry—36. Infantry, Commissariat and Military Justice—37. Artillery and Armoured Corps—38. Engineers and Technical Services—39. Medical and Veterinary Services—40. Marshal, Director of Artillery, in parade dress—41. Colonel in winter field service dress

1938 heavy 12.7 mm machine-gun developed by an engineer named Goryunov. The 1938 model gave way in 1942 to the 1938/46 model. Similar to small cannons with their shields and wheels, these two heavy machine-guns and the smaller 7.62 mm version, the Goryunov model 1943, almost completely supplanted the much-outdated Maxim. The issue of machine-guns increased by 170%.

BREN GUNS

The Degtiarev DP 7.62 mm[1] Bren gun, which saw service throughout the war, was frequently modified, until finally there was a new model, the DPM, to the same specification and with identical performance. The only differences were the tube lengthening the breach containing a recoil spring, and the addition of a pistol grip. Its rate of fire was 500–600 rounds a minute.

MORTARS

In 1941 the Soviet Army was using three categories of mortar, of 50, 80 and 120 mm calibre respectively. There were many mortars in use and during the course of the war their number multiplied. Thus while in 1941 one division of infantry could theoretically fire about 400 lbs of bombs in one salvo, four years later the weight rose spectacularly to 2,800 lbs. At this time each artillery regiment in the field had 108 120 mm mortars.

The smallest of the three 1941 models, the RM 50, was reminiscent of the old Imperial Army mortar. Its ammunition was so small that it had no effect on experienced German troops. So although it was very mobile, the little 50 mm was soon abandoned.

On the other hand, the 80 mm was very efficient and stayed in service until victory, in three successive versions distinguishable only by their different accessories and increasing ease of operation. Between 1941 and 1945 the number of 80 mms doubled.

1 See vol. 1.

There were only two versions of the 120 mm mortar, and they were very similar. This is the mortar that was copied by the Germans, whose *Granatwerfer* 42 is described in volume 2 of this series.

The 160 mm, which appeared in 1943, was specially appreciated for its terrifying efficiency against infantry assaults. By adjusting the curve of flight and making it shorter, its shells could harass the enemy from their starting point till they were almost upon the Russian lines. Soviet industry produced about 100,000 mortars of all kinds each year.

Armoured Vehicles

The Soviet Union entered the war with tanks that were either too heavy or too light, poorly armoured or too lightly armed, and for the most part out of date and with worn-out motors. Nonetheless, in only two years they succeeded in creating the most powerful armoured force the world had ever known.

Borodino in October 1941 provided the first sign of this unexpected turn of events. Here the remarkable T 34/76 with its soldered turret first appeared in large quantities.[2] The technical progress of Russian industry from this time on, put a brutal check to the Panzerdivision's hitherto irresistible onslaught. The T 34's fire power, mobility and armour-plating put it two or three years ahead of any other tank anywhere in the world.

2 Until then turrets had been riveted.

SOVIET ARMY, LIGHT ARMS

1. Tokarev 7.62 mm (1940)—2. Shpagin 7.62 mm (1941)—3. Sudayev PPS-43, 7.62 mm (1943)—4. DChK (Degtiarev-Shpagin) 12.7 mm heavy machine-gun (1938–1946)—5. Ditto, 1938 model—6. 1943 Goryunov 7.62 mm machine-gun. It replaced the old 1910 Maxim (see vol. 1)—7. 50 mm field mortar—8–10. 80 mm battalion mortars of 1937, 1941 and 1943—11. 120 mm mortar (1938)—12. 160 mm mortar (1943)

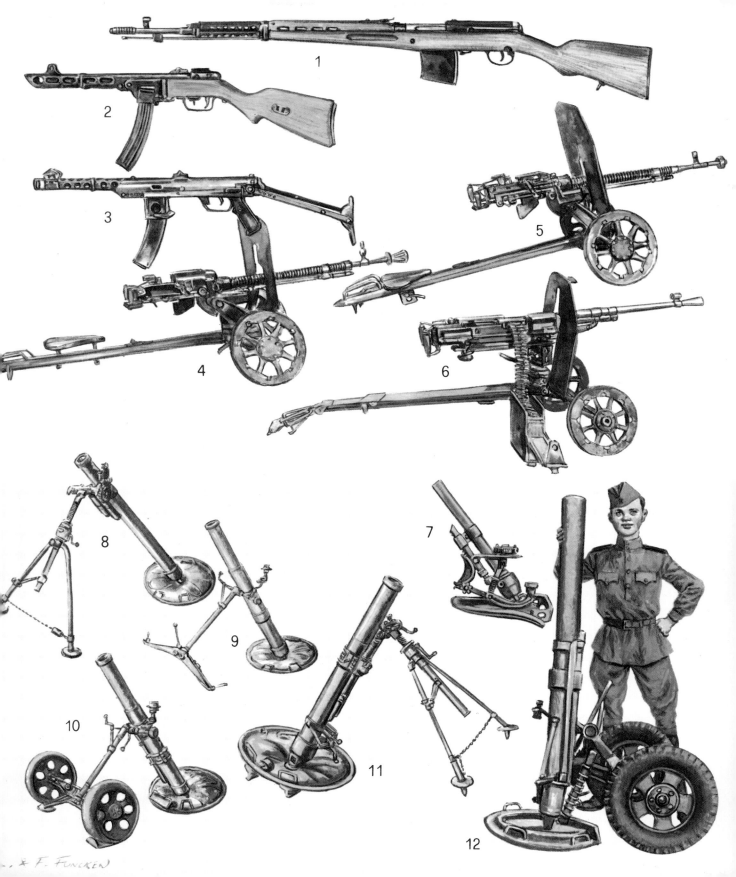

F. FUNCKEN

In the same year the model B with its hexagonal turret, longer gun barrel and speed of 20 mph, made the T 34/76 still more invincible. Finally, in the following year the model C with its little low supplementary turret for the captain gave the tank greater efficiency and more freedom of movement for the crew, who until then had been extremely cramped. When the Germans produced special tanks to fight the T 34, it was imperative to find an answer which could maintain the superiority the Russians had acquired at such cost.

So the T 34/85 came into being (the 85 being an indication of the calibre of the new cannon installed in the brand-new turret), and though one more member was added to the crew, which now totalled five, they had more space, and the tanks efficiency with its 85 mm gun (adapted from a 1939 anti-aircraft gun) was over 60% greater than its predecessor! This tank first saw battle in the winter of 1943–1944 with the crack guard units, as did all new models. It came just in time to deal with the 'Tiger' which made its first large-scale appearance in 1943. The T 34/85 went on with the fighting till Berlin, and was still in use long after the war. It was still considered as a first-class tank in 1950. On several occasions in Korea it made American soldiers beat a hurried retreat, until the British Centurion arrived and put an end to its exceptionally lengthy career.

In parallel with the T 34/85, the heavy KV series had been given a new model with a turret identical to that of the former. This one, called the KV 85 had less success in the face of the threat of new German tanks in 1943, and was used only for a year – the time needed to replace it with a far more efficient tank of the same weight, the 'Joseph Stalin' or JS.

By the end of 1943 only a few of the JS 85s had been built, and the 85 mm cannon was replaced by a 100 mm gun, in turn replaced almost immediately by a gun which had originally been designed for the artillery – a 122 mm, whose success owed more to its improved calibre than to its ballistic qualities.

It was not long before the JS 122 went into mass production, and by the end of the year the first examples of this now enormous gun, renamed the JS 1, proved to be what was needed to take on the Panther and the Tiger. The turret and step-like front were considerably modified in a second model, which came out at the beginning of 1944 – the JS 2.

The newcomer's streamlined shape made it harder to hit at right angles (the most dangerous way for a shell to hit a tank), and the armour-plating in the more exposed areas was 160 mm thick. The extra machine-gun on the JS 1 and JS 2 was just one of the characteristics inherited from the original version, the KV. By the end of 1944, 2,225 JS 2s had been built and used in all the battles of the long Eastern Front.

The Russians were holding back a surprise for the Allies – the latest model, the JS 3. It appeared during the great Allied victory parade in Berlin on 7 September 1945, but probably never had the chance to take part in the last of the fighting. A complete departure from its predecessors, the new Stalin struck observers with its ultra-modern lines, in particular the flattened 'frying pan' turret, similar to that on today's tanks.

No doubt Marshal Stalin wanted to impress his allies, who were stimulated to build a whole new generation of tanks, which appeared immediately after the war.

SOVIET ARMY, ARMOURED VEHICLES I

1. T 34/76 C, introduced at the beginning of 1942. The inscription shows that a group of farmers from the Moscow region made a voluntary contribution of this tank to the army—2. T 34/85 (winter 1943–1944)—3. KV 85. This precursor of the 'Stalin' carries the inscription 'Death to the Fascists' (winter 1942–1943)—4. JS 1 'Joseph Stalin', which entered service at the end of 1943. It bears the inscription 'Destination Berlin'. Epaulettes, collar patches and tank crew insignia are shown on preceding pages. In battle, tank crews wore dark grey or black overalls over their normal olive-green uniform

TABLE OF PRINCIPLE SOVIET ARMOURED VEHICLES FROM 1942 TO 1945

TYPE	WEIGHT	SPEED	RANGE	ARMAMENT	CREW	IN USE
T 34/76C	30 tons	33 mph	250 mls	1 × 76.2 mm cannon 2 × 7.62 mm machine-guns	4	1942
T 34/85	32 tons	32 mph	188 mls	1 × 85 mm cannon 2 × 7.62 mm machine-guns	5	Winter 1943–44
KV 85	46 tons	27 mph	206 mls	1 × 85 mm cannon 3 × 7.62 mm machine-guns	5	Winter 1942–43
JS 1	44 tons	23 mph	94 mls	1 × 85 mm cannon 3 × 7.62 mm machine-guns	4	End of 1943
JS 111	45.8 tons	25 mph	118 mls	1 × 122 mm cannon 1 × 12.7 machine-gun 1 × 7.62 mm machine-gun	4	Beginning of 1945
Self-propelled guns: SU 76	10.7 tons	25 mph	188 mls	1 × 76.2 mm cannon	4	1942–43
SU 85	29 tons	34 mph	200 mls	1 × 85 mm cannon	3 or 4	1942–43
JSU 152	46 tons	23 mph	94 mls	1 × 152 mm howitzer	4	1944

SOVIET ARMY, ARMOURED VEHICLES II

1. JS 3 'Joseph Stalin' (beginning of 1945). It is unlikely that it fought in the last battles—2. SU 76 *Samokhodnaya Ustanovka* or self-propelled 76.2 mm gun (1943)—3. SU 85 with 85 mm long gun (1943)—4. JSU 152 with 152 mm howitzer. The British called it the 'Animal Killer', referring to the numbers of 'Tigers' and 'Panthers' it destroyed. It appeared in 1944. Sometimes these Russian tanks were painted olive green with yellow ochre stains, especially in autumn

1

2

3

4

L·A·F·Funcken

SELF-PROPELLED GUNS

Long before the outbreak of war, Russia had felt the need for infantry support. After many unsatisfactory experiments, the enormous 52-ton 10 ft high KV 2[1] appeared and took part in the first battles of the 'Barbarossa' campaign in 1941.

The KV 2 was pulled back from the front, replaced by a new self-propelled gun, the SU 76. SU stood for *Samokhodnaya Ustanovka* meaning self-propelled gun. It was built on a T 70 light reconnaissance tank chassis, the first of a new generation of light tanks that appeared in 1940. Weighing 9.2 tons, with a crew of two and a totally inefficient 20 mm cannon, this little tank looked like the KV 1 and BT 7s awkward kid brother. Soon after it appeared, a 45 mm gun was put in its cramped turret, which had to be reinforced with angle irons; for all that, it was still an inefficient and vulnerable machine, and ceased to be manufactured after the spring of 1943. The chassis were saved and used for the SU 76 (76 of course referring to the gun's calibre), which was no more successful as a tank-destroyer and soon had to be relegated to the role of infantry support.

The SU 122 and the SU 152, which appeared at the end of 1942, were built on the chassis of the T 34 and the KV respectively. Rather than being used in risky confrontation with enemy tanks, both were used defensively. The SU 85 on the T 34 chassis was the first real tank-destroyer worthy of the T 34/76 in battle. Its successor, the SU 100, became the T 34/85's support in 1944.

If the reader wonders why special tank-destroyers were built, when by definition a tank is itself the best vehicle to destroy another tank, one should underline the essential difference between the two vehicles: the tank-destroyer had a fixed turret and, being larger, could carry a heavier gun than could be placed in the moving turret of a normal and smaller tank. Tank-destroyers were a valuable support and could open fire on the enemy at longer range, weakening them in the early phases of classic tank battles. As the battle progressed, tank-destroyers lost their advantage, for their fixed turrets prevented them from taking aim quickly.

The huge 40-ton JS tanks were supported by the equally heavy JSU 100, 122 and 152.

Soviet Air Power

After the terrible losses of 1941, the Soviet High Command reorganised its air force into divisions, paying special attention to long-range aircraft.

Nobody imagined that the Russian Air Force would become so powerful. Its organisation was as follows. Three planes made up a *zveno* or chain, the equivalent of our flight. Three *zvenos* made a squadron or *atriad*. The *eskadrilia*, made up of three *atriads*, was the equivalent of a French air group, that is to say, 27 to 30 planes. In bomber formations, the *eskadrilia* had about twelve planes. The development of long-range planes compensated for the logistic problems of fighting on such a long front.

The first sign of the new Soviet Air Force was the increasing frequency of Stormovik attacks. Usually flying in pairs without escort, they machine-gunned and bombed enemy positions at

SOVIET AVIATION I

1. Yak-1, original model—2. Yak-7 A (1941)—3. Yak-9 (1944), with a French Normandy-Niemen squadron—4 and 5. Yak-3 idem—6. Yak-9. The decorations painted on the nose show that the pilot held the Order of the Red Flag and was a member of the Guard—7. LaGG-3 (1942). The most common fighter in the spring of 1942, it was replaced the same year by the La-5

8. Order of Suvorov (1st class)—9. Gold star—10. Order of Lenin. These last two medals, issued simultaneously, went with the title of 'Hero of the Soviet Union'—11. Order of the Red Flag

Personal squadron insignia, common with other nations, were rare and always discreetly displayed on Soviet planes. However, they sometimes bore patriotic inscriptions such as: 'For the Fatherland', 'Fighting for the Fatherland', 'For the USSR', or a dedication from contributors: 'To Comrade X from the workers of Z'. Victories were shown by white, black or red stars, for Russians loathed soiling their planes with the emblems, however small, of the enemy they hated. This applies to armoured vehicles as well.

---

1 See volume 1 of this series.

low altitude, with both the motors and the pilots well protected by heavy armour.

There were six regiments of 'flying infantry-men' attached to the aerial corps, made up of thirty-six *zvenos* which had four or five planes each. The Stormovik started out as a single-seater, but was so vulnerable to German fighters attacking it from behind while it dived, that in 1942 a new version was built with a longer cockpit to accommodate a machine-gunner with a 12.7 mm gun to cover the rear. This new version was very efficient, for now that the pilot was freed from the worry of attack from behind, he could concentrate more efficiently on his missions of destruction.

Many were the Soviet aces who were given the title of 'Hero of the Soviet Union' after having destroyed an impressive number of tanks and other vehicles.

Fighter bombers used to attack in Indian file, flying in a circle called the 'circle of death'. This technique was used on a large scale, and one particular operation led to the almost total destruction of an entire armoured division in four hours.

The Stormovik was one of the first planes to use rockets, and when the original 82 mm rockets gave way to the 132 mm hollow charge ones, even Tiger tanks were vulnerable.

A new generation of fighters appeared at the same time as the Stormovik fighter bomber: the Yak-1, LaGG-3, Mig-1 and Mig-3. But it was particularly when the La-7 and Yak-9 appeared that Soviet airpower found itself a match for the Luftwaffe's best planes.

The La-7 was the final development of its predecessor. The name comes from that of its designer, S. A. Lavochkin, who had been made a 'Hero of Socialist Labour' for his first plane the La-5, which first saw battle in the inferno of Stalingrad in October 1942.

The La-7 had a more powerful motor and three 20 mm machine-guns and six 82 mm rockets. Ivan Koyedub and Alexander Pokryshkin destroyed 62 and 59 enemy planes respectively to become the greatest Russian aces, both flying La-7s.

In 1944 an La-7 interceptor was fitted with an extra rocket motor in the rear fuselage, so as to increase its speed for short bursts by 10 to 15 per cent, to around 470 mph. A group of these planes was attached to the *Protivovozduchnoi Oborony* or Aerial Protection Force.

But it was the Yak, designed by Alexander S. Yakovlev, which was the most justly famous of all Soviet fighters. Its enthusiastic pilots nicknamed it the *Krasavec* (Beauty). There were no less than thirteen different models of this plane, the most famous being the Yak-9 which appeared at Stalingrad in 1942.

In 1943 four new versions appeared: the Yak-9D or *Dalnii* (long-range), the Yak-9T *Tiazholy* (heavy) with a special anti-tank cannon, the Yak-9B or *Bombordirovshchik* (bomber) and the Yak-9M or *Modifikatsion* with an extra machine-gun. The classic Yak-9s principal roles were those of infantry support and keeping Messerschmitt Me-109s out of the sky (a job in which it excelled at altitudes lower than 5,000 metres). Its rate of climb was far superior to its enemy's and many an Me-109 crashed trying to follow a Yak-9 in a tight turn.

The French squadron, which served in Russia under the name *Normandie-Niemen*, chose the Yak-1 in March 1943, switching to the Yak-9 most successfully before re-equipping with the Yak-3 in October 1944.

The Yak-3 first saw battle at Kursk. It had been designed at the same time as the Yak-9 as a high-performance fighter. So successful was it that Luftwaffe pilots were officially ordered to avoid combat with it at less than 500 metres.

The last version which appeared in time to take part in the closing stages of the war was the

SOVIET AVIATION II

1. Mig-3 (1941)—2. Mig-5 (1943)—3. Tupolev Tu-25 (1943)—4. Ilyushin Il-2 M3 Stormovik (1942), nicknamed 'The Flying Trooper'. A rough illustration of the Order of Suvorov awarded to the pilot is seen on the tail fin; on the fuselage one can read 'Alexander Suvorov'—5. La-5 (1942)— 6. La-7 (1943). The decorations painted on the fuselage show that the pilot, Ivan Kozhedub, has been awarded the title 'Hero of the Soviet Union' three times. Russian fighters were extraordinarily rugged for their relatively low weight

Yak-9U, which was the first of a whole new generation: it was on a par with the best foreign planes of its kind.

The Petliakov Pe-2 was the most common and most famous of the bombers. In 1944 each of the five bomber corps had 200. Under the Lend-Lease agreement, the USSR received 15,000 planes from the United States, of which two thirds were fighters. For the most part the bombers were B-25 Mitchells and Douglas Havocs. Great Britain gave Russia more than 7,000 planes. In May 1945 the first line of the Soviet Air Force had some 17,500 aircraft.

GERMANY 1943–5, ARMY AND VOLKSSTURM

1. Soldier wearing the 1943 uniform *Feldbluse* (tunic). The ratio of rayon to wool had been increased, so that the cloth did not keep one particularly warm and was relatively fragile when wet. There are no gussets on the pockets—2. Child soldier (some were less than 12 years old!) wearing the 1944 model *Feldbluse*, consisting of a jacket and 1943 model trousers called *Rundbundhose*. The whole outfit was more grey-green than *feldgrau* in colour—3. SA Officer (see vol. 1) wearing uniform for training the Volkssturm. In battle, the military cap or *Einheitsmütze* 1943 model replaced the Nazi cap. He has a rifle with a grenade-launcher or *Schiessbecher* (*Becher* = goblet); the grenade looked like a small shell with a flattened point. On his belt he carries the honorary SA weapon—4. Member of the Volkssturm wearing the famous wooden-soled *Holzschuhe* on his feet. They were extremely comfortable in spite of their rough appearance—5. Volkssturm ranks; from top to bottom: Volkssturmmann, Gruppenführer, Zugführer, Kompanieführer, Bataillonführer—6. Traditional-style jackets made either in German sailcloth or, as shown, in Italian sailcloth (from 1943–1944)

7. VG1-5. *Volkssturmgewehr* semi-automatic 7.62 mm—8. VK 98 *Volkssturmkarabiner* 7.62 mm—9. Simplified 9 mm Erma sub-machine-gun—10. 9 mm MP 3008 without its magazine (of the same type as that shown above). As can be seen, it was a copy of the British Sten.

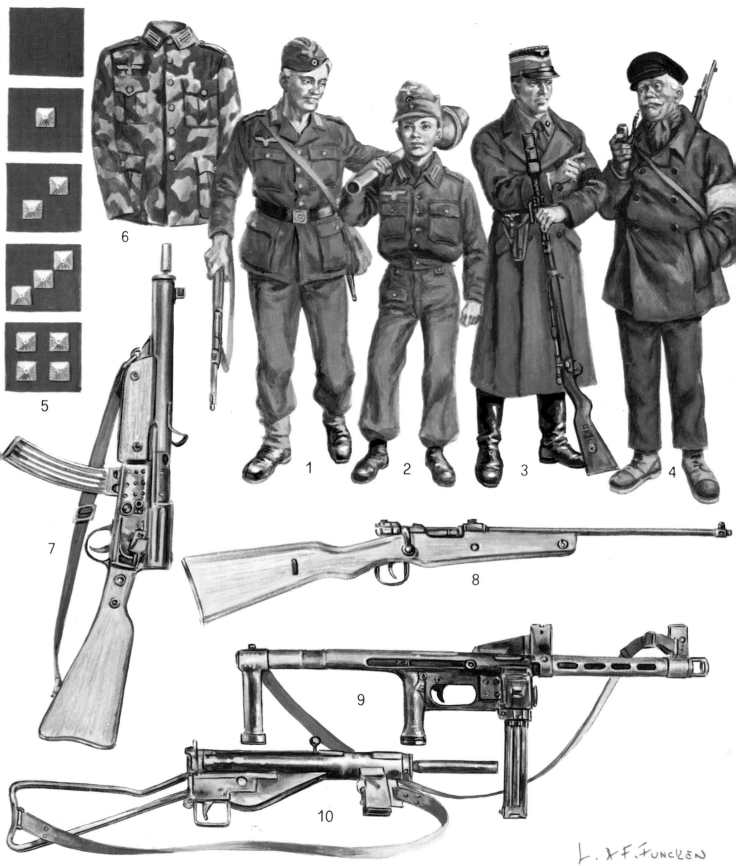

GERMANY

The Agony of the Third Reich

SOLDIERS OF FORTUNE

As a result of the total mobilisation decreed by Adolf Hitler, the *Volkssturm* was set up in October 1944. It consisted of the very last reserves that the German people could throw into battle. In it, men from 16 to 60 were grouped under the leadership of a Gauleiter, each of whom was chief of a *Gau* – the largest administrative unit of the Party and the equivalent of a county.[1]

These last-ditch recruits now began their training under the iron discipline of the Party's NCOs, who had previously been exempt from military service in order to work in administration or armaments.

Though the younger recruits fought spiritedly, their elders, many of whom had fought in the 1914–18 war, could not hide their distaste for such a blatantly suicidal tactic. Even stronger was the civilians' loathing of anything like a sniper organisation. Ever since the Franco-German war of 1870, this form of warfare had been anathema to Germans, particularly since the series of tragic mistakes in Belgium in 1914, which had led to many civilians being shot. The Germans had no illusions about the fate which awaited them.

On top of that, training took place outside the twelve-hour working day. A Volkssturm battalion did not look very imposing; apart from their rifles and gas-mask packs, the men wore their normal working clothes. Only the chiefs who were from the Party or from the SA[2] wore crossbelts and regulation uniforms.

In order to ease the troubled conscience of

this corps, shoulder badges were issued; some red, with the words 'Deutsche Wehrmacht' in black lettering, some yellow with 'Deutsche Volkssturm' in white over the word 'Wehrmacht'.

The units sent to the front received whatever uniforms were available – mainly those taken from captured countries. The uniforms of the Nazi Party's political sections were used as well, their mustard-coloured fabric being dyed with *feldgrau*, which gave them a particularly strange dark olive colour. Headgear was standardised – a mountain fighter's hat, the standard model *Einheitmütze*. Ranks were shown on the left side of the collar in the same way as the Waffen-SS as follows:

Volkssturmmann – ordinary soldier	nothing
Gruppenführer – group leader	1 star
Zugführer – platoon leader	2 stars horizontally
Kómpanieführer – company leader	3 stars diagonally
Bataillonführer – battalion leader	4 stars in a square

The Nazi High Command held no illusions about the fighting strength of these groups, but they thought that once they were in the army they would make a useful contribution. Most effective were the youths who came from schools and factories, whether fighting in the Volkssturm or in the Anti-Aircraft Corps, or, after an accelerated training programme, in the army.

GERMAN ARMY 1943–5, LIGHT ARMS

1. *Raketenpanzerbüchse* (anti-tank rocket-launcher) nicknamed 'Panzerschreck' or 'Terror of the Tanks', model 54, with projectile measuring approximately 77 mm—2. Ditto, 43 model, 88 mm with its projectile—3. How the 'Panzerschreck' was fired—4. *Panzerfaust* (anti-tank fist)—5. Its projectile; after launching, thin wooden fins unfold to stabilise it—6. How the *Panzerfaust* was fired—7. *Maschinenpistole* 44, more accurately known as the *Sturmgewehr* (assault rifle) 44, an extraordinary weapon—8. The MP 44 could use a system for firing around corners, to get at enemies in concealed positions or mounted on a tank—9. Attachment for firing around 45 degrees, called 'Krümmerlauf' (elbow gun), with a periscope for street fighting. Ammunition fired through these devices usually came out in fragments

1 See details of uniforms and organisation in volume 1 of this series, pages 55–60.
2 See volume 1, pages 60–3.

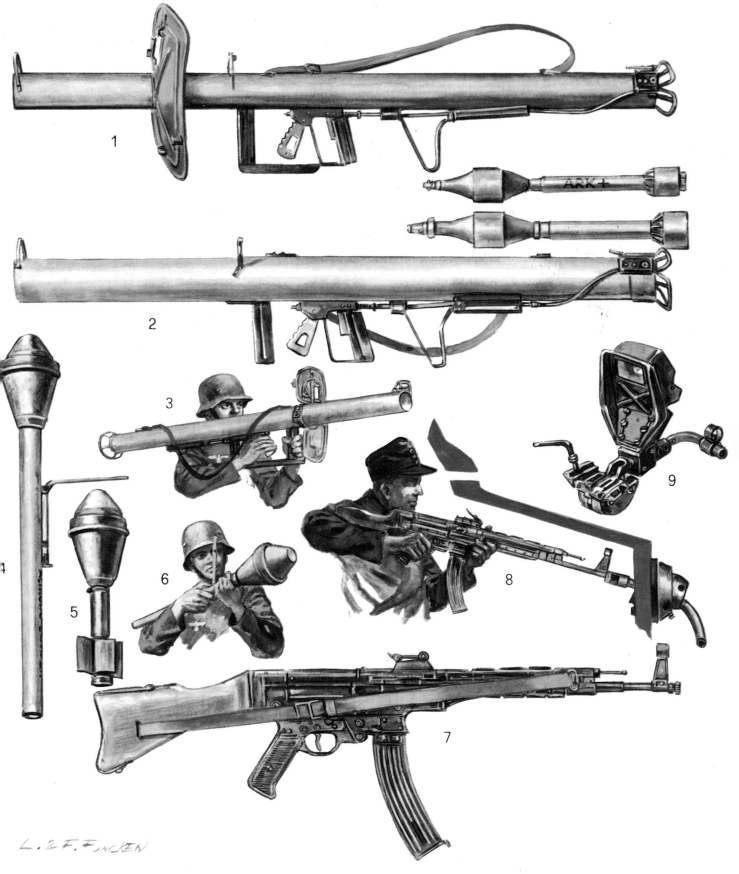

1

2

3

4

5

6

7

8

9

ARK 1

L. & F. Funcken

WEAPONS

Popular assault troops had two kinds of rapidly produced weapons. The first was the VG 1 or *Volkssturmgewehr* 1 rifle, with a magazine from the Model 43 semi-automatic rifle. It had been put into production so quickly that it was somewhat hazardous to use. It had the same 7.92 mm calibre as the VK 98 or *Volkssturmkarabiner* 98 carbine – a far better gun made from old carbine parts.

The VG 1–5 was a semi-automatic rifle similar to the Bergmann, Schmeisser or Beretta sub-machine-guns, with a classical wooden butt.[1] Surprisingly enough it does not seem to have been tested or approved by the *Waffenamt*.[2]

The MP (*Maschinenpistole*) 3008 sub-machine-gun was a copy of the famous British Sten, but more extraordinary was the EM 44 Erma, which was made of soldered tubes and looked very strange. Cheap and easy to manufacture, it does not seem, however, to have been made in quantity.

MORE MODERN LIGHT WEAPONS

Of the last weapons produced by the Germans, the most remarkable was, without doubt, the *Sturmgewehr* 44 – an infantry rifle oddly named the MP (*Maschinenpistole*) 44. It fired the standard short round automatically or semi-automatically and was so successful that the Russians copied it for their new automatic rifle.

The real revolution in infantry weapons was the rocket-launcher based on the American bazooka. Colonel Dörnberger, the V2 specialist, developed the *Raketenpanzerbüchse* 54, better known as the *Panzerschreck* (tank-terror) and nicknamed *Ofenrohr* (stovepipe). But it was largely replaced by the little grenade-thrower called the *Faustpatrone* (fistshot), also known as the *Panzerfaust* (anti-tank fist), which fired a hollow charge grenade. These were quite different from the *Panzerschreck* rockets and were simply fired by exploding a charge in the breach of the launching tube. There were four types of *Panzerfäuste*: the *Faustpatrone* 1

1 See volume 1, pp. 76, 77 and 80.
2 Weapon service

with a 30-yard range, the little *Panzerfaust* 30 called 'Gretchen' (Margot), which was lighter but had the same range, the *Panzerfaust* 60 which could fire over 30, 60 and 80 yards, and finally the heavy model 100, which had a range of 150 yards. In the hands of first-rate soldiers, these weapons destroyed a good many tanks and were used to a far greater extent by the Germans than by any other troops.

German Armoured Vehicles

Despite the appearance of large numbers of new Tiger and Panther tanks, the summer of 1943 saw the beginning of a general retreat by the German forces in Russia.

Defeat at Stalingrad and increasing Soviet pressure posed enormous problems for the German

GERMAN ARMY, ARMOURED VEHICLES I

1. Model G 'Panther'. Although this tank's arrival halted Russian T34s from the end of 1942, nonetheless it was not until the 'Tiger' appeared that they were outclassed—2. Tiger II 'Königstiger' (1944) with original model turret and 88 Kwk 43 gun—3. 'Hetzer' (huntsman) self-propelled gun and tank-destroyer with 1944 Pak 39 75 mm gun—4. 'Sturmtiger' with shell-lifting crane and 380 mm RW 61 rocket-launching mortar. This could fire almost vertically; the holes visible round the muzzle allowed excess gas to escape during firing

5. Uniform of the 'Hermann Göring' Panzerdivision. The traditional black uniform was worn with plain white collar patches and black epaulettes, with piping in the colour of the branch of the army. An armband with silver lettering worn at the bottom of the right sleeve shows the unit's name. Note the Luftwaffe eagle on the cap. One should perhaps explain how the 'General Göring' Air Regiment (cf. vol. 1) became an armoured division. This regiment (later, in the summer of 1942, a brigade) was turned into an 'HG' Panzerdivision in January 1943. Decimated in Tunisia the following spring, it was reborn in Italy (June 1943) and fought in Sicily. In January 1944 it became the 'Fallschirmjäger-Panzerdivision HG' (armoured parachutists' division). Having fought against the Allies at the Nettuno landing, it was sent to Russia in July. Divided into two corps ('Fallschirmjäger-Panzergrenadierdiv. HG' and 'Panzerkorps HG'), it was annihilated while trying to halt the Russian advance

1

5

2

3

4

L. & F. Funcken

High Command, particularly as on the Western front the recent Anglo-American and Free-French victories in North Africa brought ever closer the threat of an invasion of 'Fortress Europe'. Meanwhile, British and American bomber squadrons were dropping more and more bombs on German factories.

Only a new attack against Russia could chase away this spectre of final defeat for the German High Command. There was no question of this operation being a mortal blow to the Russian forces, only a means of checking them and allowing the armies of the Reich to retake the initiative.

Besides, if the plan succeeded, it would have a beneficial effect on army and civilian morale, seriously shaken by a long series of reverses. The OKW[1] believed too that victory here would cause a serious and perhaps permanent split between the Anglo-Americans and the Russians, whose coalition was already fragile.

It must be remembered that the Reich still had at the time an enormous military potential: its factories had never produced so much in the way of ammunition – so many guns, tanks, and planes – sufficient not only to replace losses but also to equip new units, and as it seemed unlikely that the Anglo-Americans would open a second front, the Germans could commit almost all of their forces to the Eastern Front.

Paradoxically, the retreat in February had been a strategic success since it shortened a front which had been far too spread out. In spite of everything, the Russians had succeeded in breaking through in three places: in the north between Leningrad and Lake Ladoga, south of Moscow, at Kursk and at Kharkov, which the Germans had recaptured. The town of Kursk, about 240 miles south of Orel and north of Kharkov, made a narrow salient cutting into the German lines, called the 'Kursk Salient'.

Hitler decided, with faultless logic, to attack this salient in a pincer movement with his troops in Orel and those in the Kharkov area. The opera-

tion was called 'Citadel' and the Führer stressed the importance of its success, saying that it must shine out on the world like a lighthouse beam.

The two armies were enormous:

German Army	Russian Army
Soldiers: 900,000	Soldiers: 1,300,000
Field guns: 10,000	Field guns: 20,000
Armoured vehicles: 2,700	Armoured vehicles: 3,300
Planes: 2,500	Planes: 2,600

The battle began on 5 July, but it was not until the 12th that the greatest tank battle in history began. The Russians called it the 'Battle of Kursk'. For seven days two armies of armoured vehicles grappled with each other in a duel which had to end decisively, one way or the other.

The Germans had pinned their hopes on the Tiger and Panther tanks, and the Ferdinand[2] tank-destroyer. Apart from the Panther, these machines were vastly superior to any other tank in existence, but technical progress, however remarkable, was not enough to compensate for the numerical superiority and heroism of the Russians, who had no hesitation in paying a price unacceptable to any other nation in order to win their victory. The battle was an inferno in which tanks fired at each other at point-blank range and some, in flames, hurled themselves on their enemies.

The Wehrmacht suffered the heaviest defeat in its history, losing its last 'Battle for Victory' with disastrous consequences for its prestige. 'Operation

2 Later renamed 'Elephant'; see volume 2, page 112.

GERMAN ARMY, ARMOURED VEHICLES II

1. Jagdpanzer IV (1944) with Pak 39 75 mm gun. It also had more powerful guns like the long 75 mm gun of *Kampfwagenkanone* 42 and the 75 mm *Sturmpanzerkanone* 42 nicknamed the 'Guderian Duck'—2. Jagdpanther (Hunting Panther) with 1944 model 88 Pak 43 gun. There was another version identical to the above, apart from the armour around the gun mounting, which was narrower and had a larger bulge. Jagdpanthers were the strongest of all tank-destroyers— 3. Jagdpanzer VI Jagdtiger (1944) with a Pak 44 128 mm gun. It could also fire the 88 Kwk 43. Although powerful, it suffered from poor manoeuvrability and was the heaviest armoured vehicle in the German army, though there were only a few in the *Heerespanzerabteilungen*

1 *Oberkommando* (Headquarters) *der Wehrmacht.*

1

2

3

L. & F. Funcken

TABLE OF PRINCIPAL GERMAN ARMOURED VEHICLES FROM 1943 TO 1945

TYPE	WEIGHT	SPEED	RANGE	ARMAMENT	CREW	IN USE
PzKpfw VI Tiger II or *Königstiger* (Royal Tiger)	70 tons	25 mph	105 mls	1 × 88 mm cannon 1 × 7.92 mm machine-gun	5	1944; 485 in service
Jagdpanzer VI *Jagdtiger* (tank destroyer Hunting Tiger)	71.7 tons	22 mph	62 mls	1 × 128 mm cannon 1 × 7.92 mm machine-gun	6	1944; only a few
Jagdpanzer Tiger 'Elefant' (ex-'Ferdinand')	68 tons	22 mph	50 mls	1 × 88 mm cannon 1 × 7.92 mm machine-gun	6	1943; 90 built
Sturmpanzer *Sturmtiger* (Attacking Tiger)	68 tons	?	?	1 × 380 mm mortar 1 × 7.92 mm machine-gun	5	1944; 18 built
Jagdpanzer 38 *Hetzer* (Huntsman)	16 tons	25 mph	112 mls	1 × 75 mm cannon 1 × 7.92 mm machine-gun	4	1944; 1,577 built; used as combat tanks and tank destroyers
Jagdpanzer V *Jagdpanther* (Hunting Panther)	45.5 tons	34 mph	130 mls	1 × 88 mm cannon 1 × 7.92 mm machine-gun	5	382 built; the strongest of all tank-destroyers
Sturmpanzer IV *Brummbär* (Grizzly)	28.2 tons	25 mph	125 mls	1 × 150 mm howitzer 1 × 7.92 mm machine-gun	5	1943; in very limited quantity

Citadel' lasted for five days and losses on both sides were enormous. It is not possible to give exact figures, for both sides claimed quite outrageous numbers of enemy tanks destroyed, more than there were on the whole field of battle. Nonetheless it can be estimated that the Germans lost 2,000 armoured vehicles, for with the Russian breakthrough they did not have time to repair immobilised tanks. The Russians, for their part, could recover a good part of the 1,500 to 2,000 Soviet tanks which had been damaged.

The battle of Kursk was the first summer victory for the Red Army, and put paid to the legend that Russian soldiers could win only in winter with the cold on their side. From now on the Soviet advance was to confirm this trend.

GERMAN ARMY, ARMOURED VEHICLES III

1. Tiger 'Elefant' also known as 'Ferdinand' after its designer, Ferdinand Porsche. The ribbed textured effect (which can also be seen on some of the previous illustrations), which covered the tank up to 6 ft above the ground, was designed to prevent the magnetic charges of enemy infantry becoming attached—2. Sturmpanzer 'Brummbär' (Grizzly). Two of the five pieces of armour plating can be seen. They were used on the majority of German tanks. (See vol. 2, p. 110)—3. Sd. Kfz. 302 or *Sonderkraftfahrzeug* (special motor vehicle) Zündapp B1 'Goliath' with radio-controlled electric motor, seen with its two-wheeled transporter. There was an identical Sd. Kfz. 303 which had a motorcycle motor controlled by a set of cables. These remote-controlled devices were first used at Anzio, but were found to be very vulnerable

1

3

2

L. x F. FUNCKEN

SUPER CHAMPIONS

After the Panther, the first tank to have any success against the terrible Russian T 34 and to prove a match for American Shermans, the Tiger was another unpleasant surprise for the Allies.

The Tiger II which followed, fortunately in small numbers, was without doubt the most powerful tank of its time. The Elephant tank-destroyer based on the Tiger II was less successful. To start with, it had no defence weapons for close combat, and was often (particularly at Kursk), destroyed by Soviet infantry. Although it was better protected later, this *Jagdpanzer* was still heavy and unmanoeuvrable; it is significant that it was most efficiently used in ambushes when it was covered with camouflage netting.

The impressive 'Sturmtiger' was destined to destroy especially difficult targets, but it was so vulnerable that it could only be used where the infantry had already won control.

The Germans tried to use existing chassis on many occasions and were successful with the 'Hetzer', based on a Czechoslovak tank, and particularly the 'Jagdpanther', based on the Panzer IV which, having a low silhouette and sweeping lines, was very difficult to hit, while its fearful 88 mm gun could destroy any of its enemies.

The 'Goliath' or 'Zündapp BI' is the best known of the remote-control demolition vehicles. There were two versions – the more important, the B IV, looked like a little Bren gun carrier, and was more than twice the size of the Goliath: nearly twelve feet long and radio controlled, this machine had a detachable explosive charge and could come back to its starting point, before the explosion. An intermediate model, the NSU 'Springer' (Jumper) worked the same way, but all these devices needed exactly the right set of circumstances, and because they were so lightly armoured, were very tricky to use.

German Air Power

The winter of 1943–1944 was a decisive turning point for Germany, and the beginning of a series of trials and tribulations which would lead to her collapse.

The fighters trying to contain the growing tide of enemy bombers suffered enormous losses. General Galland, the head of fighter command, wrote in a report to Hitler: '. . . Our fighters are outnumbered seven to one. . . . In the course of the last four months (December 1943–March 1944) we have lost more than 1,000 pilots including our best squadron leaders and wing commanders. These losses can no longer be made up. . . . We have reached the stage where the complete collapse of German fighter command is a possibility'.

The fact that such overt pessimism should be expressed by one of the real heroes of the Luftwaffe confirms the opinion of one of the great French pilots, Pierre Clostermann, who reckoned that only 15 to 20 per cent of the German aces were of higher standard than the average Allied pilot, and that the remaining 80 to 85 per cent were really not much good despite their courage, for these young pilots had been trained too quickly, and were unable to make the best of their superb aircraft.

GERMAN AVIATION

1. Me-163 B Komet. It deserved its name, for at take-off it shot out a 50-ft flame from its exhaust nozzle. Hans Liska, the famous draughtsman, created a badge for the Me-163 squadron showing Baron Münchhausen—2. Bachem Ba-349 Natter (Viper). Its only test flight ended in a fatal accident—3. Arado Blitz (Lightning Flash). The first jet bomber (beginning of 1945)—4. Heinkel He-162A Salamander or Volksjäger (February 1945)—5. Me-262A 2a, Schwalbe (Swallow) in its fighter version or, as here, Sturmvogel (Stormbird) in its bomber version. In May 1945 six of these planes destroyed twelve Flying Fortresses in one dog-fight—6. Developed from the famous Focke-Wulf Longnose, the Focke-Wulf 152 TA was flying with only a few squadrons at the time of the surrender. TA stands for its inventor, the engineer Kurt Tank—7. Me-410 Hornisse (Hornet), more than 1,600 of which were introduced in 1943. In spite of very heavy armament, its performance never justified its use on such a large scale

All the same, German fighter pilots were never of a higher standard than that reached by the end of 1944 and the beginning of 1945. In his book *Le Grand Cirque* Clostermann explains this paradox, claiming that from 1944 the Germans abandoned the system of rotating the best squadrons from the Western front to the Russian front – where quantity rather than quality was needed – so that they could stay and defend their homeland against the devastating Anglo-Saxon air forces.

The German aircraft industry's revolutionary new planes arrived too late and in too small numbers to affect the situation.

The Focke-Wulf Longnose 190 D appeared in 1943 and was an unpleasant surprise for Allied fighters. The Messerschmitt 262, the first jet fighter to be used effectively and on a large scale, was even more dangerous. But Hitler had slowed up production so as not to hold up the manufacture of traditional aeroplanes, and then insisted despite experts' objections that the majority of Me-262s be converted into bombers. When this foolish order was countermanded in October 1944, it was too late.

There were other newcomers in the Luftwaffe which saw active service – the little Me-163 rocket plane, a development of the Kraft-Ei (Mighty Egg) designed by Alexandre Lippisch, and the Heinkel 162 Salamander or Volksjäger, which Hitler planned to crew with a future Hitler Youth air force, and which was one of the most extraordinary planes. However only the Me-163 scored more than a dozen kills.

Rockets

Having hoped for so long to win a victory with traditional weapons, Hitler now turned to the rockets that some of his scientists had been working on in the greatest secrecy.

Hermann Oberth's remarkable successes in 1925 were based on the experiments carried out by the Russian Tsiolkovsky and the American Goddard. The rocket test centre at Kummersdorf was set up in 1932 and its importance grew from year to year.

The first two rockets were able to reach 6,000 ft by 1935, and from then on more and more money was spent on research.

It was only after many years and many unsuccessful tests that the first truly convincing launch of a rocket to a height of 250,000 ft took place on 3 October 1942. The 'Aggregat 4', forerunner of present-day missiles, had been born. It became known in its final version of the V2 (V for *Vergeltungwaffe* – revenge weapon) and 5,000 were built. It is worth while remembering that Wernher von Braun, now famous for his work at NASA, was one of the men responsible.

While work was going on with rockets, another group of scientists was set to work by the air force to design a flying bomb powered by a pulse-jet engine, also known as a Schmidt tube after its inventor, who had perfected it in 1934. It was called the 'Fieseler 103' or V1 and first flew in 1941. There was strong rivalry between the Luftwaffe's V1 and the army's V2, but in the end, both were pressed into service, the better to wage

GERMANY, ROCKETS

1. V1. Total weight: 2 tons (1,400 lbs of trinitrotoluene and ammonium nitrate explosive and one ton of crudely refined petroleum propellant). Maximum range: 250 miles. Speed: approximately 400 mph—2. V2. Total weight: 13 tons (1 ton of explosives and 9 tons of alcohol and liquid oxygen propellant). Speed at take-off: 1,000 ft per second; at impact: four times the speed of sound. Range: more than 250 miles—3. 'Rheinbote' rocket. Although nearly 30 ft long, this rocket carried only 80 lbs of explosives and used a dry propellant—4. Henschel Hs-293 radio-controlled flying-bomb, nicknamed 'Buck Rogers'. It weighed 1 ton and carried 1,300 lbs of explosives at a speed of 400 mph—5. FX-1400, nicknamed 'Fritz 1400'. The first radio-controlled missile, it flew at 625 mph—6. One of the six kinds of bomber which could launch these terrible new bombs was the 'Kondor'. The bomb was carried under the left wing as shown—A. V2 trajectory. For ease of reading, height is shown on a scale ten times greater than range. (cf. real trajectory A1). At D, the rocket motor shut off, at 95,000 ft—B. Trajectory of V1—C. Trajectory of A-4b rocket, a winged version of the V2 which, fortunately, never got beyond the test stage. E and F show contemporary altitude records in an aeroplane at 56,000 ft in 1938 (Lieutenant-Colonel Pezzi, an Italian); and in a balloon: 72,500 feet in 1935 (Carl David Anderson, an American scientist)

IONOSPHÈRE

100 Km

90

80

1

70

60

2

50

A

40

3

STRATOSPHÈRE

30

D

F

20

4

6

10 TROPOPAUSE

TROPOSPHÈRE

5

A₁

B

C

L. de F.Funcken

0   100 Km   200   300   400   500   600   700   800

Hitler's total war. V1s began to bombard England from 13 June 1944. 2,000 had been launched by the end of the month, 8,000 by September and 10,500 by 1945. Fortunately nearly 4,000 flying bombs were destroyed or crashed into the sea. The first V2 fell on London on 8 September 1944. England was to receive over 2,000 more.

Now that the German forces were retreating and Great Britain was no longer within range, their targets were on the continent: Antwerp alone was hit by 1,600 V2s and nearly 200 'Rheinbote' rockets.

The Hs-293 and the FX-1400 flying bombs were launched from aeroplanes. The former was used at least once in the Mediterranean against the British fleet, while the latter was used with great success when one direct hit sank the Italian battleship *Roma*.

A whole new arsenal of far more powerful rockets was being tested when the war ended.

ITALY

The Fascist Army 1943–1945

Mussolini was overthrown two weeks after the Allied invasion of Sicily on 10 July 1943. He was arrested and moved from the island of Ponza to Maddalena,[1] and finally was locked up in a hotel,

1 Ponza is on the gulf of the Gaeta between Rome and Naples. Maddalena is between Sardinia and Corsica.

the Campo Imperatore, at Gran Sasso, 7,000 ft up in the Abruzzis. That his *alter ego* should be subjected to such humiliation was intolerable for Hitler, who ordered his rescue. Otto Skorzeny, the famous SS officer, carried out this mission with rare bravery on 12 September.

Meanwhile, the King of Italy had asked Marshal Badoglio to form a new government, and above all to get Italy out of the war. On 3 September a secret armistice was signed with the Allies

ITALY, TROOPS OF THE SOCIALIST REPUBLIC

1. Grenadier—2. Parachutist. On the right, special badge for beret. Lapel badges as fig. 26—3. Militiaman of the National Republican Guard in ordinary winter dress—4. Sailor from the San Marco Division—5. Soldier in a Black Brigade of the *Corpo ausiliario delle squadre d'azione delle Camicie nere* (Blackshirts)

Collar patches (mostrine) 6. *Arditi* (assault group) of the San Marco Division—7. Alpine troops. On the right, above: Alpine horse artillery. Below: Alpine anti-tank detachment—8. Bersaglieri—9. Grenadiers—10. Cavalry—11. Artillery—12. Engineers—13a. Appennine Light Infantry—13b. Alpine Light Infantry—14. Divisional veterinary company—15. *Volontari di Sardegna* battalion, the first formation in the new Republic, wearing the Sassari brigade's colours—16. M (Mussolini) assault battalion—17. Collar flash and epaulette of a sergeant in the Littorio Infantry Division with German braid (Germany 1944)—18. Italia Infantry Division. Note the badge in a vertical position. National Republican Guard:

19. Public Order—20. Fascist Youth—21. Assault battalion—22. Italian Waffen-SS (it was probably never worn, see vol. 2)—23. Battalion of young volunteers, *avanguardisti*, 'White Flame'—24. Air force cap badge—25. Anti-aircraft artillery—26. Parachutists—27. San Giusto Armoured Squadron—28. Navy cap badge—29. Ship-borne troops—30. Land troops—31. San Marco Naval Infantry Division. Behind: artillery of the same division—32. San Marco coastal battery—33. San Marco assault group. Auxiliary police of the Socialist Republic: 34. E. Mutti legion in the Black Brigade—35. Political Police dealing with suppression of anti-Fascists

36. Emblem of the new army, seen on many *mostrine*. Arms badges: 37. *Arditi*—38. Alpine—39. Bersaglieri—40. Grenadiers—41. Cavalry—42. Artillery—43. Engineers and Appennine light infantry

44 and 45. Mussolini armoured group. As far as one can tell, in spite of the creation of new badges, the old *mostrine* in the form of a hammerhead still survived in a good many cases

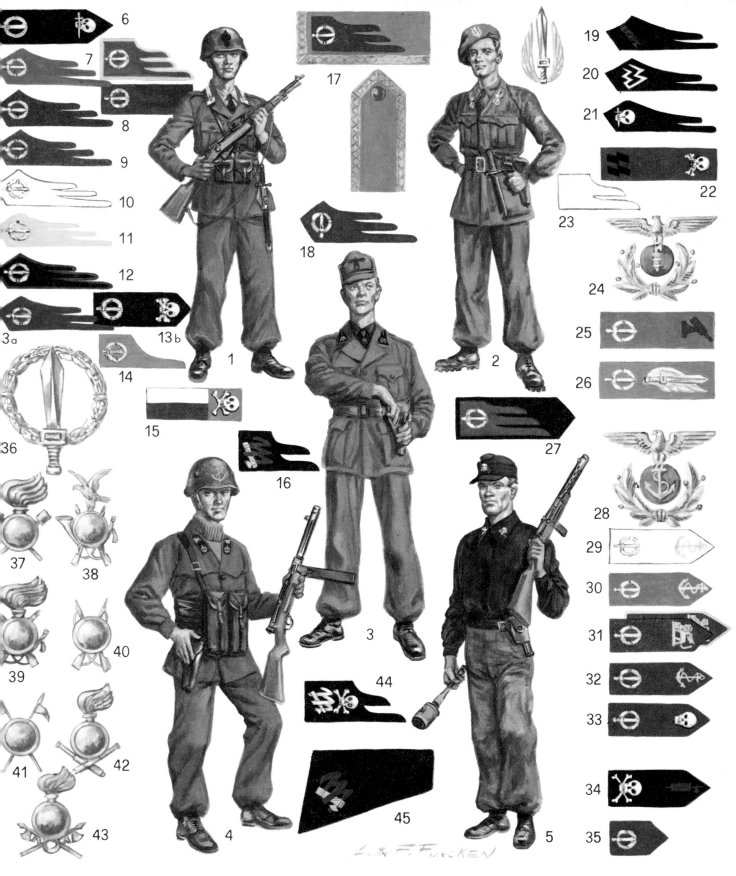

to be officially proclaimed on the 8th in a radio communiqué. That night the King, Badoglio and most of the general staff fled towards Brindisi, away from German reprisals. But the Germans had long suspected Italy's intentions, and had long since taken charge of all places of strategic importance. They disarmed all thirty Italian divisions in Italy, the twenty-five divisions scattered through the Balkans and the 4th Army which was in southeast France. Receiving no orders, 700,000 Italian soldiers were herded into cattle wagons and transported into captivity in Germany. In Saxony it took twenty-four hours for these columns of *Badoglio Truppen*, as the captured soldiers were sarcastically named, to pass by, marching ten abreast.

The Germans brought the *Duce* back to Italy. Now an old man, he took charge of the new Fascist Republic, the 'Repubblica Soziale Italiana' at Salo on Lake Garda, for the Germans would not allow him to go to Rome.

It was many months before Nazi Germany allowed the formation of the Republican Army. At last Mussolini was allowed to set up and train four divisions on German soil. They were supposed to be made up of volunteers drawn from the prisoner-of-war camps, but so absurdly small was their number that men had to be conscripted from the last third of Italy still under Fascist control.

However there were so many deserters that of the 180,000 called up, only 40,000 entered the army or *Guardia Nazionale Repubblicana*, whose main job was fighting the partisans. 50,000 more young men were deported to the Reich to work in the factories. The German military administration or *Militärverwaltung* treated the *Duce* with thinly disguised scepticism and confiscated everything that the Socialist Republic produced, from shoes to trucks, asking them to pay for the cost of their occupation. These Fascist soldiers were most active in the fighting against the partisans, during which atrocities reached unparalleled heights.

UNIFORMS

The Republican troops mostly wore safari jackets with *mostrine* sewn on to identify the unit. Traditional Italian headgear was worn, though often replaced by 'Panzer' berets or *Einheitmütze* in various colours. The Italian hat had the ancient Alpine, Grenadier, or naval unit emblems stencilled on. In 1945 the infantry wore German hats with the national coat of arms on the right, and the Fascist eagle drawn in a thin black outline on the front. Summer uniform was a light khaki canvas. Arms and equipment came from old stocks.

Volunteers and Partisans

Having survived the enormous débâcle of the armistice, some Italian units were led on by their officers to fight the Germans. For example in Corsica the 7th Italian Army Corps took part in the liberation of Bastia, losing 500 men. In Greece, when the Acqui division rebelled, it lost 4,500 officers and soldiers. Lastly, in northern Italy, small units regrouped and formed the kernel of various partisan units.

The first regular Italian units, set up under Allied auspices from December 1943, fought hard. It was only in June 1944, thanks to the *Corpo Italiano di Liberazione* volunteers, that Italians were able to play an important part in the liberation of their country.

Uniforms came from Great Britain: traditional battledress with concealed or visible buttons, with khaki berets for land troops and black for

ITALY, PARTISANS AND REGULAR TROOPS

1–3. Soldiers in the *gruppi di combattimento* of the *Corpo italiano di liberazione*. Fig. 3 is a bersaglier—4. San Marco Regiment with the lion of St Mark on the sleeve cuffs. It will have been noted that the same units existed in the Fascist army, shown on the preceding page, another example of the absurdity of this Civil War—5–8. Volunteers and partisans

the navy. Once again the famous *mostrine* and traditional regimental insignia were used, sometimes with a ribbon coloured red, white and green on the left arm.

When the *Giustizia e Libertà* divisions began to fight on a large scale in September 1943, the partisans fought the fascists openly. From the spring of 1944 General Cardona's Freedom Volunteer Corps joined forces with the Garibaldi Brigade and the Patriotic Action Groups. They had some 200,000 men ready to emerge from their mountain hideouts at any moment to attack convoys or isolated guard posts, or to blow up railways and bridges.

The partisans tried to look like a regular army with their quantities of Italian light arms . . . and they sometimes succeeded. There seemed to be inexhaustible supplies of the ever-popular safari jackets which came in many colours: khaki, tan, brown or grey-green. Depending on whether or not the volunteers had served in the Royal army, military headgear varied from the traditional forage cap to the Alpine hat with its single feather. Inspired by regular troops, the Resistance forces sometimes sewed a ribbon with the battalion tricolour on their left sleeve carrying the letters CVL, standing for *Corpo Voluntari della Libertà*. But one piece of clothing showed their political 'colour' most precisely – a green, red, or sky-blue neckscarf.

It was some red-scarfed partisans from the Garibaldi Brigade who found Mussolini cowering at the back of a German truck dressed in a German greatcoat and hat. On the shores of Lake Como on 28 April 1945 a burst of machine-gun fire from 'Colonel Valerio' deprived the Allied courts of the pleasure of passing judgment on the ex-Dictator.

PART TWO

THE SMALLER NATIONS
DENMARK AND THE NETHERLANDS

Denmark

Despite the non-aggression treaty signed with Germany on 31 May 1939, little Denmark had no illusions, and when war broke out in the west in September she was determined to defend herself.

Though he had promised to respect her neutrality, Hitler soon realised that Denmark constituted a vital corridor for his armies to invade Norway. The German attack took place on 9 April 1940 at 4 am, ostensibly to protect Denmark from ... an imminent British invasion!

Only the Danish navy was on the alert, but it was unable to prevent two German ships entering the port of Copenhagen and capturing the fort. At the same time troops landed in various places along the coast, while others crossed the frontier.

It has often been said that Denmark gave up without firing a shot. However, on the border and in front of the royal palace at Amalienborg, Danish soldiers opened fire. These were no doubt minor skirmishes, but nonetheless deserve to be recorded. Knowing full well that the British and French could not intervene, the government was forced to accept Denmark's occupation.

The Nazis' unwarrantable intervention in Danish political life infuriated those patriots who refused to see their country integrated into a 'new Europe'; the few who supported the Reich formed a *Frikorps Danmark* to fight Bolshevism on the Eastern front. Sabotage was on the increase in 1943, with its inevitable corollary, capital punishment. The *Schalburgkorps* were to clean up the Resistance networks, and their cruel repression finally led to an uprising in Copenhagen in June 1944. Denmark was liberated on 5 May 1945, but the last German islands held out until 7 May.

UNIFORMS

Denmark had no illusions about its little army's efficiency in the face of attack, and its defence budget was minuscule.

During the First World War, uniforms had been changed to the dull colours universally adopted. In Denmark's case stone grey was chosen. In 1923 a new khaki uniform was issued, but only to the officers and senior NCOs, other ranks keeping their old grey uniform, so that the Danish army was probably the only two-coloured army in the world.

The medieval-shaped 1923 helmet and the 1926 gas mask were the only items common to both uniforms, apart from the black coat, which was an 1864 model, and the 1870 model trench shovel. It is astonishing that in spite of this mixture, Danish soldiers looked more modern than many soldiers from more powerful countries.

The Netherlands

On 10 May 1940 the Netherlands were brutally invaded by General von Bock's troops striking simultaneously in four places in the north and at The Hague, Rotterdam and Zeeland. The XVIIIth German Army under General von Küchler consisted of one armoured division, one parachute division, two cavalry divisions and ten infantry divisions.

The Dutch army consisted of:
four army corps, each consisting of two infantry divisions, one regiment of light infantry, one regiment of artillery and ancillary services;
one light division of two cycle regiments, two regiments of motor-cycle hussars, one machine-

gun squadron, one artillery regiment and 24 armoured vehicles;

one mixed brigade of two infantry regiments, one artillery regiment, one machine-gun company and one company of engineers.

Never was the name *Blitzkrieg* more aptly applied than to the five dark days from 10 to 15 May, all the time Germany needed to destroy the Dutch army.

10 May: The taking of the bridge at Moerdijk (near Dordrecht) and the airfield at The Hague by parachute troops. Ground forces reached the Groningen–Nijmegen line. In the south troops crossed the Meuse between Roermond and Venlo.

11 May: The enemy storms the Ijssel defences and approaches the Grebbe.[1] To the south they crossed the Peel marshes to reach Tilburg and Bois-le-Duc.

12 May: Breakthrough of the Grebbe line; the enemy reaches Amersfoort and Dordrecht.

13 May: The 9th Panzer Division and the 2nd 'Das Reich' SS Division slaughter Dutch troops who have surrounded German parachutists at Rotterdam. Rotterdam is severely bombarded.

14 May: Utrecht attacked and threatened with the same fate as Rotterdam. In the south, Dutch defences are taken from behind.

15 May: With open towns threatened by massive bombardment, and realising the hopelessness of the situation, General Winkelman orders his exhausted and decimated troops to lay down their arms.

Some Dutch troops kept fighting until 17 May in Zeeland, shoulder to shoulder with the 60th and 68th French Divisions.

---

1 A small tributary of the Rhine on the north bank, the Peel marshes stretch from the limit of Dutch Limbourg to northern Brabant.

THE DUTCH NAVY

Though far from being a naval power of the first order, the Dutch navy was second to none when it came to sailors. We have a tragic example of their exemplary courage when the Japanese

DANISH ARMY

1. Officer—2. Infantryman in the new uniform—3. Infantryman with old uniform and equipment

Cap badges: 4. Generals—5. Senior Officers—6. Subalterns—7. NCOs—Arms badges worn on the lapel by officers and NCOs: 8. Commissariat—9. Officers—10. Health—11. NCOs—12. Veterinary—13. Armoury

14. 8 mm Krag model 1889/10 rifle

Ranks: 15. General—16. Lieutenant-General—17. Major-General—18. Colonel—19. Lieutenant-Colonel—20. Captain—21. Captain-Lieutenant—22. 1st Lieutenant—23. Lieutenant—24. 2nd Lieutenant—25. Company Sergeant-Major 1st class—26. Sergeant-Major 2nd class—27. Sergeant-Major 3rd class—28. Sergeant-Major 4th class—29. Staff Sergeant—30. Sergeant—31. Cadet—32. Corporal—33. Soldier 1st class

NETHERLANDS ARMY (pages 64–5)

1. Officer of infantry of the line in ceremonial dress (1940)—2. Light infantry officer in ceremonial dress (1940)—3. Officer in the Hussars (1936)—4. Naval Officer—5. Horse Artillery (1940)—6 Air Force officer (1940)—7. Foot Artillery (1940)—8. Hussar (1936)—9. Light infantryman (1940)—10. Sailor in tropical landing uniform (1940)—11. Infantry Colonel (1942)—12. Machine-gunner in the infantry of the line (1940)—13. Grenadier (1940)—14. Machine-gunner (1940) of infantry of the line—15. Schwarzlose 6.5 mm machine-gun of infantry of the line—16. Detail of helmet badge. The colours of arms could be seen on collar and facings. Grenadiers: red; light infantry: green; infantry of the line and engineers: blue; hussars: light blue; artillery and pontoneers: dark red

17. Paw M.39 (for *Pantserwagen*) armoured car with three 6.5 mm machine-guns and a 37 mm gun. In 1940 the firm DAF had produced twelve of these

Ranks: 18. General—19. Lieutenant-General—20. Major-General—21. Colonel—22. Lieutenant-Colonel—23. Major—24. Captain—25. 1st Lieutenant—26. 2nd Lieutenant—27. Sergeant-Major (in the place of the star there was a round button)—28. Sergeant-Major—29. Sergeant 1st Class—30. Quartermaster—31. Sergeant—32. Corporal. Navy: 33. Admiral—34. Vice-Admiral (Commodore)—35. Vice-Admiral—36. Rear Admiral—37. Captain—38. Commander—39. Lieutenant-Commander—40. Lieutenant—41. Ensign 1st class

attacked the Pacific possessions that gave Holland third ranking in the world as a colonial power.

Admiral Karel Doorman and the Dutch East Indies Naval Division were overcome fighting heroically against the enemy fleet on 27 February 1942, off Java.

THE BALKAN AND DANUBE STATES

Bulgaria

It is time now to say a few words about countries on the other side of Europe . . . while trying not to get caught up in the confusion of the Balkans.

Following her defeat in 1918, Bulgaria obtained permission to rearm after having signed a non-aggression pact with her neighbours. But she immediately hurried to claim back the province which the Allies had obliged her to cede to Rumania in 1919. With German help, this claim was upheld in 1940, and the German army got permission to enter Bulgarian territory for an eventual attack against the traditional common enemies, Greece and Yugoslavia. In exchange, Hitler promised Bulgaria a part of the territory once these countries had been crushed.

Curiously enough, Bulgaria never declared war on the USSR, even when the latter seemed on the point of surrender in 1941. However, King Boris III (1918–1943) declared war against Great Britain and the United States. Bulgaria only joined the tripartite pact (Germany–Italy–Japan) after her neighbours Hungary and Rumania had done so; and as with them, from that point her independence was illusory. Bulgaria only played a very minor part in the war, and when in September 1944 the Russian advance threw the country into the allied camp, the army was placed under Russian command and fought the Germans in Yugoslavia, Hungary and Austria.

Hungary

On the eve of the German invasion of Yugoslavia, the Hungarian government joined the tripartite pact, signing at the same time a 'Treaty of Eternal Friendship' with the Yugoslavs. Once the latter had collapsed at the beginning of the war, Hungarian troops were sent to conquer the territories lost after 1918.

In order to have a share in the bounty that Germany was giving Rumania, Laszlo Bardossy's government, using the pretext of a mysterious bombardment, rightly or wrongly accused the USSR of aggression, and declared war on 27 June 1941.

BULGARIAN ARMY

Ranks: 1. Major-General—2. Colonel—3. Captain—4. Lieutenant—5. Captain in the Health Service—6. Sergeant-Major—7. Lance-Sergeant—8. Soldier 1st class—9. Soldier (infantry, distinctive sign: red)—10. Artillery—11. Cavalry—12. Engineers

13–15. Air force officers and soldiers. The stretched false chin strap shown in fig. 14, taken from an actual photograph, shows well how unfashionable and somewhat wretched were the majority of Bulgarian soldiers at the time—16. Officer in field service dress—17. General in full-dress uniform—18. Artillery officer in field service cap and greatcoat—19. Infantryman in field service dress—20 and 21. Officer and soldier marching in summer field service dress. The soldier's epaulettes are in khaki cloth. He wears a bastardised version of the German helmet, differentiated in particular by its increased height

The Bulgarian air force was small, and occupied mainly in defending the Rumanian oilfields and patrolling the Black Sea. In 1943 it received some 120 French Dewoitine fighters which the Germans had captured. Later it received Me-109s to fight in Russia

A first expeditionary corps set off in the summer, returning to Hungary in the autumn. But from the beginning of 1942, Germany insisted on a more than token participation. 200,000 men equipped by the Reich moved off towards the Russian front and in January 1943 found themselves in the frozen Voronezh sector, together with Italian Alpini corps and German soldiers from the B Army. In the middle of a violent snowstorm some of these Hungarian units were encircled together with their allies by General Moskalenko's forces.

Two Hungarian divisions attached to the 2nd Army had the same fate a little further to the north near Kastornoye, on the same field where in 1919 Budennyy had beaten the white cavalry.

The Russian troops under General Golikov were unable to encircle them completely, but here as in the Voronezh sector the Hungarians were practically exterminated; the few who escaped lost all their equipment.

So half-hearted was Hungary's collaboration, that Hitler had the country occupied in March 1944 and the new government recruited forces for the Eastern front.

Having fought under the hardest conditions, the last Hungarian troops still faithful to Germany fought inside surrounded Budapest until 13 February 1945, then retreated towards Germany together with a million refugees.

Rumania

One of the most astonishing paradoxes of the Second World War was Rumania's siding with Germany, when during the 1914–18 war she had fought so heroically with the Allies.[1]

It is true that the country was totally isolated at the beginning of the war and that Hitler had taken advantage of this in forcing a series of concessions from King Carol II, forcing the Rumanian economy to work for the Reich. This had been done with the help of Rumanian sympathisers of

1 See volume 1 of *Arms and Uniforms: The First World War.*

German origin in Transylvania where they were one of the most vociferous minority groups. They had set up an organisation based on Fascist and Nazi militias called the Iron Guard.

The most characteristic item of their uniforms was the green shirt, green being meant to symbolise the hope which only the 'truly patriotic' soldiers had.

Though apparently Germany's vassal, not only the army but also the majority of the Rumanian people showed many signs of hostility. The government had to call on Rumanian army officers

HUNGARIAN ARMY

1. Marshal—2. Lieutenant-General—3. Major-General—4. Brigadier—5. Colonel—6. Lieutenant-Colonel—7. Commandant—8. Captain attached to the general staff—9. Lieutenant attached to the engineering staff—10. Sub-Lieutenant—11. Artillery cadet—12. Battalion Sergeant-Major (rapid troops)—13. Adjutant—14. Quartermaster-Sergeant—15. Sergeant—16. Staff Sergeant—17. Corporal—18. Soldier 1st class—19. Ordinary soldier (fusilier or light infantry)—A green background on collar tabs meant infantry. Narrow gilt epaulettes were worn by everyone from Marshal to officer cadet. Below this rank, epaulettes were of the colour of the arm with black piping and no other decoration—20. The manner in which the above ranks were shown on the left sleeve of greatcoats

Air force: 21. Air Vice-Marshal—22. Air Commodore—23. Colonel—24. Lieutenant-Colonel—25. Commandant—26. Captain—27. Lieutenant—28. Sub-Lieutenant—29. Cadet—30. Colonel attached to the General Staff—31. Air force engineer Lieutenant-Colonel—32. Technical Staff Major (Air force)—33. Battalion Sergeant-Major—34. Adjutant—35. Quartermaster-Sergeant—36. Sergeant—37. Staff Sergeant—38. Corporal—39. Soldier 1st class—40. Ordinary Soldier

Field service caps: 41. Generals—42. From Colonel to Cadet—43. Light Infantry—44. Infantry (here an adjutant)—45. Mountain Light Infantry shown with visor extended—46. Detail of badge which was gilt (as shown here) for officers, silver for NCOs and bronze for soldiers. Note the rich beauty of the badges, rarely equalled elsewhere

47. General in service dress—48. Quartermaster-Sergeant in full-dress uniform—49. Infantry Captain in field service dress—50 and 51. Infantrymen in field service dress—52. Soldier in the River Fleet. On the left, detail of badge—53. Air force soldier—54. Pilot officer—55. Captain in winter flying suit. Badges of rank were worn on the sleeve in rectangles. Above, detail of cap and beret badge. As with the River Fleet, this badge was gold for officers, silver for NCOs and bronze for soldiers. Pilots also wore a similar badge on the chest, with horizontal wings

to be more friendly to the German instructors sent to reorganise the armed forces.

Placed entirely under German command, the Rumanian army fought on the Eastern Front from 1941 to 1943, on the Prut, the Dniester, in the Crimea, from the Don to the Volga, in the Caucasus and on the Sea of Azov. Of the 1,000,000 men called up, 600,000 were killed.

The hatred of Germany felt by the army and people was in no way diminished by the annihilation of the 20th Infantry Division and the 1st Cavalry Division at Stalingrad. In the beginning of 1944 when the Russian advance forces were pushing towards the Rumanian frontier and enemy units were cut off from each other, many Rumanian soldiers tried to cross over to the enemy. After four months of calm, on 20 August the Russians attacked the Germano–Rumanian positions along the frontier, forcing them to give way. On the 25th the 3rd Rumanian Army was caught in a pincer movement and was forced to lay down its arms. On the 24th King Michael of Rumania had the leader of the Iron Guard arrested, formed a new government, and declared that his country had retired from the war. The next day Rumania declared war on Germany and the whole army rebelled, attacking German forces everywhere, and preventing even the capture of Bucharest that Hitler had ordered.

General Managarov and the 53rd Russian Army entered the capital on 31 August without firing a shot. The 'Tudor Vladimirescu'[1] divisions that the Russians had organised were among those taking part in the victory parade.

Yugoslavia

The Prince Regent, Paul, had signed the tripartite pact allying Yugoslavia to Germany and Italy. This alliance guaranteed Yugoslavia's frontiers and promised her the Port of Salonika as soon as Greece had been occupied.

1 A hero of Rumanian Independence in 1821.

But two days later, on 27 March 1941, the population of Belgrade demonstrated to protest against this collaboration with the Nazis and, with shouts of 'War rather than the Alliance!', overthrew the government and placed the 18-year-old prince on the throne. Young King Peter II and his prime minister, Air Marshal Simonovic, a pastmaster of coups d'état, called for a general mobilisation to begin on 30 March.

Hitler's answer was a thunderbolt. On 6 April he attacked in force in six different places along the frontiers with Austria, Hungary, Rumania and Bulgaria, reinforced with Italian troops, and invaded the 'rebel' territory. The 300,000 poorly equipped soldiers of the Yugoslav army had been mobilised too late to hold back the flood-tide of 650,000 troops.

RUMANIAN ARMY

1. Soldier in field service dress. The old Adrian-style helmet was still being worn—2. General. Superior officers wore the Rumanian star on their cap with a crown surrounded by gold laurel leaves. Subalterns had a grenade (infantry), a horn (light infantry), or crossed cannons (artillery), in gold on a blue ground with the crown and gold laurel leaves—3. Officer in the Mountain Light Infantry—4. Soldier wearing a képi. Artillery and cavalry sometimes wore darker trousers—5. Palace guard—6. Naval petty officer—7. Air force officer—8. Air force corporal

Ground force ranks: 9. General—10. Lieutenant-General—11. Major-General—12. Colonel—13. Lieutenant-Colonel—14. Major—15. Captain—16. Lieutenant—17. Sub-Lieutenant—18. Battalion Sergeant-Major—19. Quartermaster-Sergeant—20. Sergeant—21. Staff Sergeant—22. Corporal—23. 1st class—24. 2nd class—25. Regiment of the Guard (officers)—26. Light infantry (officers)—27. From top to bottom: technical troops, light infantry, artillery, palace guard—28. From top to bottom: cavalry, infantry, administration, engineers—29. From left to right: health service, veterinary, pharmacy—30. From top to bottom: frontier guards, tanks, gendarmerie, commissariat

Navy: 31. Admiral—32. Lieutenant—33. Officers' lapel badge

Air force: 34. Air Vice-Marshal—35. Wing Commander—36. Colonel—37. Lieutenant-Colonel—38. Major—39. Captain—40. Lieutenant—41. Sub-Lieutenant—42. Lieutenant Engineer—43. Battalion Sergeant-Major—44. Adjutant—45. Quartermaster-Sergeant—46. Sergeant—47. Staff Sergeant—48. Corporal—49. 1st class—50. Mechanics Sergeant-Major—51. From top to bottom: fighters, bombers, anti-aircraft artillery, searchlights

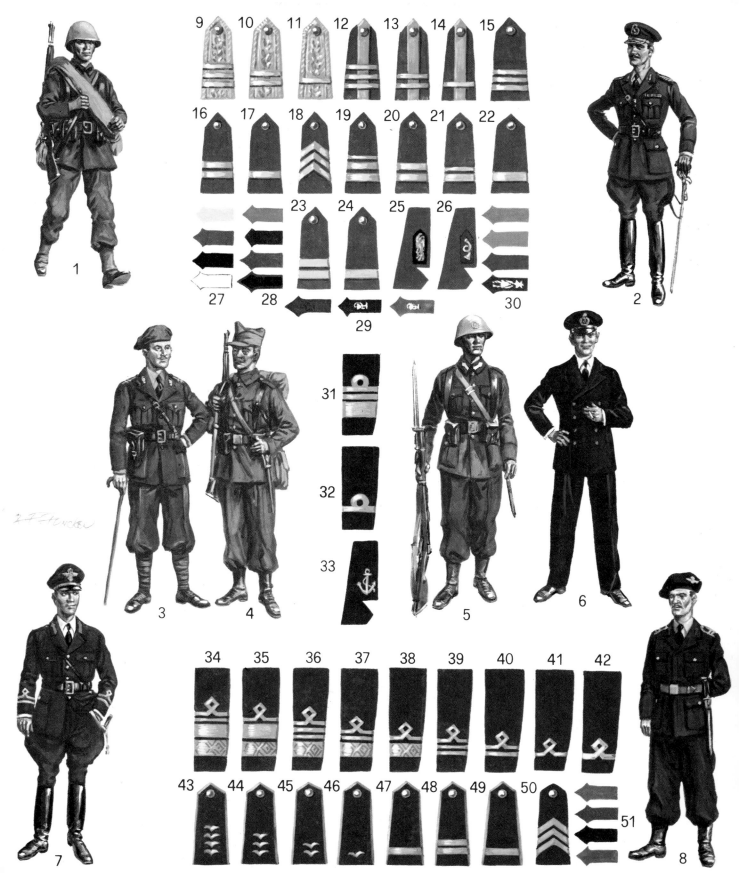

Yugoslavia's injudicious plan of campaign caused them heavy losses from the start, while the military potential of Peter II's army was not increased by the defection of three Croatian battalions at full strength.[1] On 11 April five Hungarian brigades invaded Yugoslavia encountering no opposition apart from some civilians with outmoded rifles. The result was inevitable.

On 14 April the majority of the Yugoslavian army was beaten, and the country surrendered three days later; after eleven days of fighting 254,000 soldiers had surrendered to the Germans who had lost only 151 men. The government fled to Egypt with 15,000 soldiers, a few ships and a handful of planes.

The Resistance movement began almost immediately, in two separate forms – the first organised by General Mihajlovic was Royalist; the other, Communist, was led by a civil engineer, Josip Broz, called 'Tito' because he used to give his orders in the informal second person singular.

Tito's partisans and Mihajlovic's 'chetniks' were united for a short period, but soon ideological differences and their leaders' diametrically opposite visions of their country's future forced them apart. Still worse, Mihajlovic, thinking that the time was not yet ripe, made a secret agreement with Nedic, the Croat general whom the Germans had placed at the head of the recreated country of Serbia – an agreement under which the 'chetniks' were no longer to be disturbed.

Soon resistance became civil war, and Mihajlovic's partisans joined the Italian anti-guerrilla actions against Tito. The government in exile in London could no longer support such behaviour and General Simonovic used the radio to urge his compatriots to rally under Tito against the Royalists.

The German High Command were forced to respect the partisans' courage and skill. In the end Marshal Tito had 500,000 men and was able to hold off five German attacks. His men lived under the strictest discipline: theft, looting and drunkenness were punishable by death.[2]

1 See volume 3 of this series.

2 Here we should like to mention the small state of Albania, which Mussolini invaded on 7 April 1939 with an army of 100,000 men, reinforced by the navy and the air force. The *Duce*'s action was in response to the 'provocations' of King Zog, who had repulsed commercial agreements and had refused the establishment of an Italian base. Weak and ill-prepared, the Albanian army could withstand no more than a few localised encounters before it collapsed. The army of occupation raised fourteen battalions for the fight against the partisans, whose first groups had appeared towards the end of the year, and these were then ordered to join in the attack on Greece.

YUGOSLAVIAN ARMY

1. General—2. Lieutenant-General—3. Major-General—4. Brigadier, here attached to the general's staff—5. Colonel—6. Lieutenant-Colonel—7. Major—8. Captain 1st class—9. Captain 2nd class—10. Lieutenant—11. Sergeant-Major—12. Adjutant—13. Sergeant-Major—14. Sergeant—15. Corporal—Figs 5–12 are in the bright red of the infantry. The cavalry had blue, artillery and engineers black, and commissariat green

Air force: 16. Sub-Lieutenant—17. Lieutenant—18. Captain—19. Captain 1st class—20. Major—21. Lieutenant-Colonel—22. Colonel

Navy: 23. Sub-Lieutenant 2nd class—24. Sub-Lieutenant 1st class—25. Lieutenant 2nd class—26. Lieutenant 1st class—27. Lieutenant-Commander—28. Commander—29. Captain—30. Rear Admiral—31. Vice-Admiral—32. Admiral—Arm badges: 33. Chief petty officer—34. 2nd class petty officer—35. Sailor 2nd class

36. Artillery General—37. Cavalry subaltern—38. Officer and soldiers in battledress—39. Flying officer—40. Sailor

L. & F. FUNCKEN

Greece

Mussolini, wishing to show his independence of Germany, decided to attack Greece on 28 October 1940. He was sure he could conquer this little nation of 6,500,000 people with ease. What pretext was to justify such naked aggression? 'Not having the attitude expected of a neutral state' and, more concretely, the Greek government's refusal to have Italian troops in Greece 'for purely defensive reasons'.

With hardly any modern vehicles, the Greek army could muster only one cavalry division against five armoured or motorised divisions, 17 infantry divisions against 63,160 planes and 27 warships against an omnipotent navy and airforce.

The Italian offensive began with immense confidence, and should have put the most astonishing German victories in the shade. But, alas for Mussolini, three weeks later Greek counterattacks pushed the enemy back across the frontier. By the end of the year the situation was even worse, for the Italians had been pushed forty miles into Albania. The Fascists launched a vigorous offensive from 9 to 15 March 1941, in which 30,000 more soldiers were killed or wounded with no gain.

In one of the blackest periods of its military history, at the same time Italy lost the battle of Sirrenia in North Africa.

The Axis powers' prestige was brought to ridicule by the new Caesar's misfortunes, and on 6 April Hitler decided to intervene. While his soldiers invaded Yugoslavia, he attacked Greece with two assaults south of Yugoslavia, and five others well spaced out along the Bulgarian border. The Métaxas and Aliakhom lines were broken and overrun.

The British, hurrying to the rescue from North Africa, could not stem the German tide and had to fight a vigorous retreat. The exhausted Greek army had to surrender after an 18-day battle.

GREEK ARMY

1. Lieutenant-General—2. Colonel—3. Lieutenant-Colonel—4. Major, here attached to the staff—5. Captain—6. Lieutenant—7. Sub-Lieutenant—8. Quartermaster-Sergeant—9. Sergeant—Chevrons worn on the arm: 10. Corporal—11. Sergeant—12. Quartermaster-Sergeant—Colours of arms worn on the collar: 13. Infantry—14. Cavalry—15. Artillery—16. Engineers—17. Transport, officers and soldiers—18. Health service, ditto—19. Gendarmerie, ditto—20. Commissariat officer

Navy: 21. Admiral of the fleet—22. Admiral—23. Vice-Admiral—24. Rear Admiral—25. Captain—26. Commander—27. Lieutenant-Commander—28. Lieutenant—29. Petty officer 1st class—30. Petty officer

31. Mountain artillery officer with chevrons of reserve NCO—32. Infantryman with old-style Adrian helmet—33. Evzone with English helmet—34. General—35. Subaltern—36. Infantryman with new-style helmet—37. Naval officer

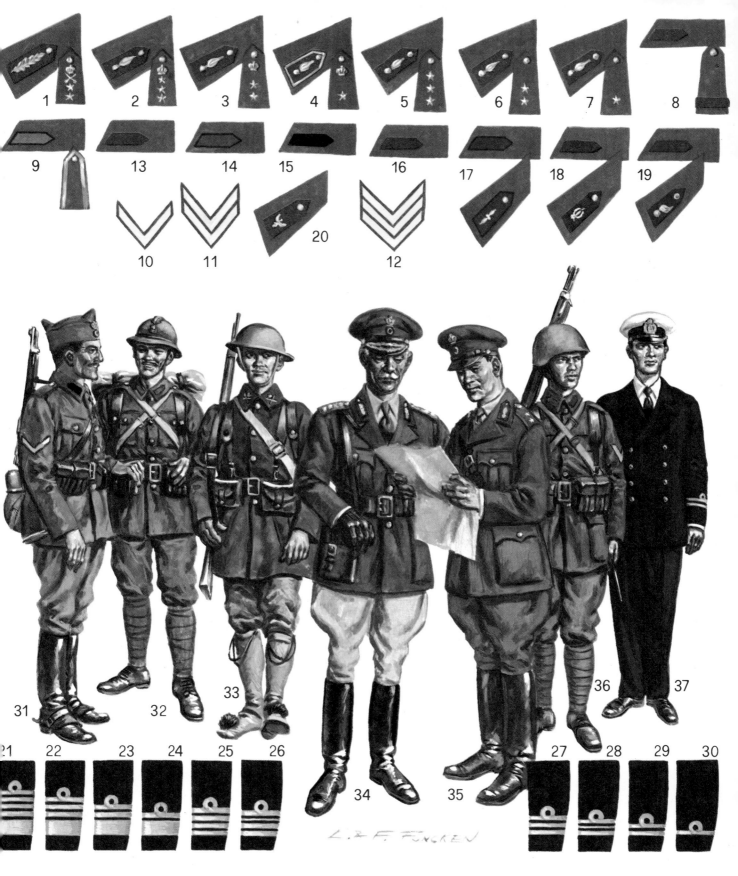

1

2

3

4

5

6

7

8

9

13

14

15

16

17

18

19

10

11

20

12

33

31

32

34

35

36

37

21

22

23

24

25

26

27

28

29

30

L. & F. FUNCKEN

PART THREE

TECHNOLOGICAL DEVELOPMENTS
ARTILLERY

Traditional Artillery

So many light and medium artillery weapons from 75 mm to 125 mm calibre were used in the Second World War that it would be impossible to enumerate them all here.

The Germans entered the war with a huge number of this kind of gun, but also with an astonishing choice of 150 mm and 170 mm motorised guns, with a 210 mm cannon or mortar, a 210 mm on tracks, 240 mm and 280 mm cannons or howitzers as well as the enormous 305, 320, 420, 560, 600 and 800 mm.

The Russians used their 45, 76.2 and 122 mm guns on a massive scale. On 19 November 1942 the 5,000 guns at Stalingrad fired 700,000 rounds on a day now known as the 'artillery day'. At Kursk there were 20,000 guns and at Berlin 22,000.

The British and Americans had their 25-pounder, the 105 mm M2 and the famous 155 mm Long Tom. In Italy they were firing an average of 20 to 30 rounds for every German round. After D-Day the Americans fired enormous quantities of shells: 300,000 rounds were fired on Aix-la-Chapelle and 132,000 in 4 hours to cross the Ruhr. Patton's 3rd army alone used 6,000,000 rounds. The United States had 9,000 artillery pieces in 1940, but by 1945 she had more than 600,000 guns.

Anti-Aircraft Guns

The best anti-aircraft guns in 1939 were without doubt the Germans' famous 88 mm and its big brother the 128 mm, which made flying over Germany a nightmare for Allied pilots. The small

20 mm and 37 mm rapid-fire guns made life hard for fighter planes at low altitudes. According to statistics, 20,000 rounds were needed to destroy a single plane. As the guns improved, this figure fell to 4,000 rounds; these relatively poor figures can be explained by the fact that designers paid little attention to the higher speed and altitudes flown by modern planes.

A 90 mm gun similar to the German 88 was grudgingly adopted in France, because the muzzle velocity caused such rapid wear that the army preferred to stick to the outdated 75 mm, which could fire thousands of rounds. The British 94 mm was a normal calibre adaptation of similar characteristics. It was slightly superior to the American 90 mm. The Russians chose a very high quality 87 mm anti-aircraft gun.

In spite of the deluge of shells it produced, anti-aircraft fire was somewhat inefficient, at any rate at the beginning of the war. It was altogether too expensive for the Belgian anti-aircraft units. The Brussels group had three batteries of four 94 mm Vickers guns bought from Great Britain with the help of private funds. No fuseborers had been sent with these superb guns, for they were considered top secret so the volunteers and reservists in the GTA (*Garde Territoriale Antiaerienne*) had to improvise a way of judging the range at which their shells should explode. The results were astonishing: when an enemy plane flew through

TRADITIONAL ARTILLERY I

1. French 105 mm howitzer—2. Japanese 70 mm 1922-style howitzer—3. Belgian 120 mm model 31 gun—4. English 25-pounder howitzer (87.6 mm)—5. German 105 mm howitzer. The standard divisional artillery piece, this gun was also used on a Panzer II chassis for the 'Wespe' self-propelled gun (see vol. 2, p. 98, fig. 8)—6. The German artillery's classic heavy howitzer, the 210 mm

the barrage of heavy Anglo-French anti-aircraft batteries nearby, Belgian Vickers guns were already loaded with shells that had been fused for the estimated height of the intruder. Three successive salvos were fired. It was rare for an enemy aircraft not to be shot down in this way. During the short Belgian campaign, Lieutenant Stievenart's[1] little battery alone knocked out 17 enemy aircraft; the French commandant was amazed and called across to his opposite numbers: 'Hey there, are you aiming?'

Short-Range Rockets

In 1940 American scientists took up where British research had left off on the development of guided rocket shells. The rocket built in 1941 was officially called the VT rocket (Variable Time and Vacuum Tube). It had a tiny radio receiver transmitter, working off a miniature battery (as suggested by W. A. S. Butemant the British scientist). As soon as launching had switched on the transmitter, it began sending out radio waves. When it was close enough for its target to reflect them back, the charge would explode.

At sea, VT rockets increased the efficiency of the anti-aircraft units by 400%; in Europe they were most successful against the V1 and German infantry.

The short-range rocket was without doubt the Allied arsenal's no. 1 weapon. Only the absolute secrecy surrounding its use can explain its relative lack of recognition.

One of its inventors said sadly that if all the time, money and scientific brains devoted to creating this weapon of war had been used in the cause of peace, the majority of mankind's problems could have been solved.

1 This resourceful officer was killed when Soviet planes bombed the camp at Prenzlau.

Anti-Tank Guns

The inefficiency of anti-tank guns in 1939 and 1940 is clearly shown by the German army's first victorious campaigns.

Just about all the armies at that time thought that 25 mm to 37 mm calibre guns were quite heavy enough. But as we pointed out in volume 1,[2]

2 See pages 118 and 120.

TRADITIONAL ARTILLERY II

1. Russian 76.2 mm 1939 gun—2. American 105 mm howitzer—3. 155 mm M2 gun called 'Long Tom' (USA)—4. Russian 203 mm howitzer. Uniforms shown are the second type issued in 1943

ANTI-AIRCRAFT ARTILLERY I (page 80)

1. 88 mm Flak 41. This was the most famous German anti-aircraft gun; previously there had been 3 types, the Flak 18, 36 and 37—2. 128 mm Flak 40 (Germany)—3. 90 mm American gun. 2,000 of these were built each month from 1942. Although not as good as the German 88 and the British Vickers, the 90 mm did well, particularly once the proximity fuse round had been introduced. The soldier in the foreground shows the standard issue US Army haversack —4. 75 mm French. There were many versions, all equally inefficient, as the designers tried in vain to adapt First World War guns which had not been designed as anti-aircraft guns—5. M.38 quadruple 20 mm (German)—6. German Flak 38 20 mm. The shield shows the silhouette of planes hit and the date of each

ANTI-AIRCRAFT ARTILLERY II (page 81)

1. Russian 37 mm automatic—2. British Vickers 94 mm— 3. British 40 mm Bofors. This was originally a Swedish gun— 4. British mobile radar. The word 'radar' comes from *RAdio Detection And Ranging*

5. How a radar station worked. Born of Sir Robert Alexander Watson-Watt's researches in 1935, radar was working perfectly by 1940, and saved Great Britain. A. Permanent radar scanning of the sky. Once an enemy plane is spotted, radar B is alerted—B. This radar follows the enemy aircraft, signalling radar C—C. This radar worked as a range-finder, recording speed and altitude of the enemy plane and communicating this information to the fire director at D—D. The fire director sent the relevant information to the anti-aircraft gun batteries—E. Anti-aircraft batteries—Of course in reality the different components in this plan were much farther apart and the aeroplane usually flew at a much higher altitude

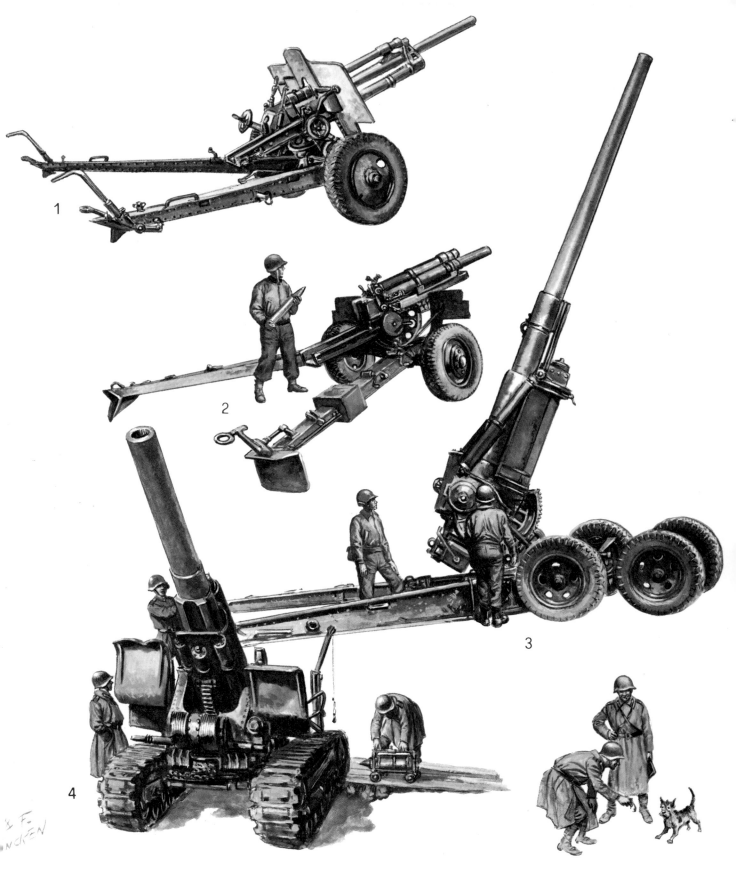

1

2

3

4

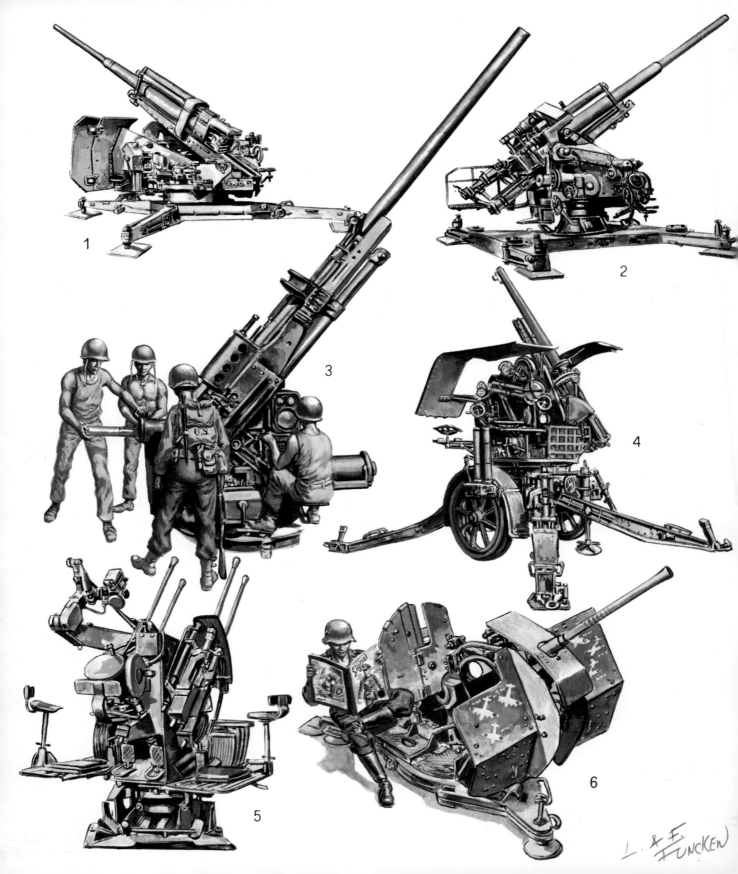

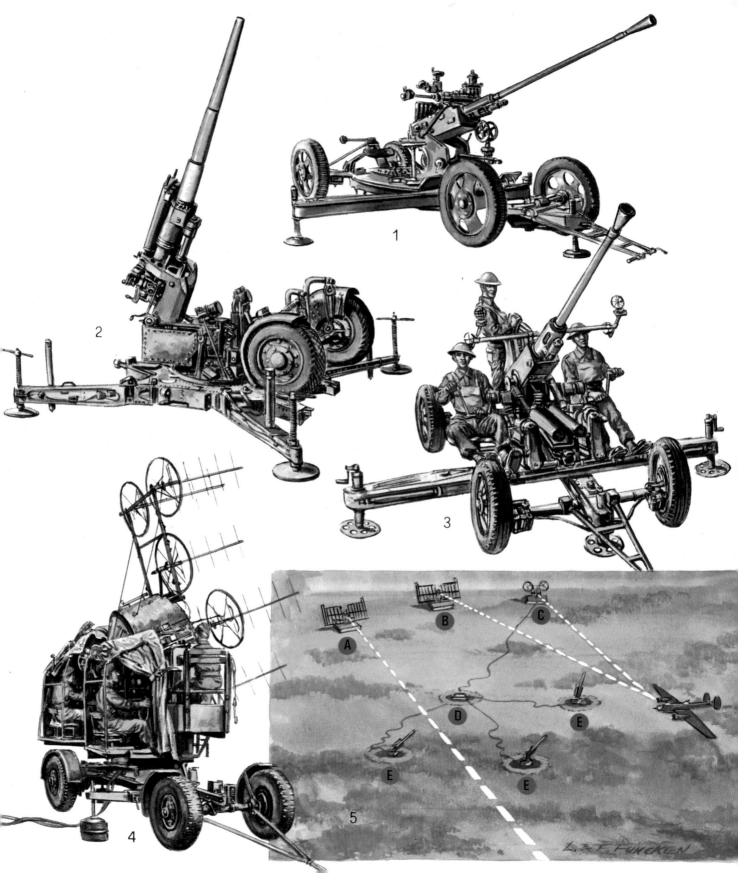

1

2

3

4

5

A

B

C

D

E

E

E

L.F.Funcken

there was an enormous difference between the circumstances in which tests took place and actual combat. A few of those countries who were to be involved in the war, such as Belgium and Rumania, were aware of their defects and chose 47 mm guns instead, as a stronger defence against the latest armoured vehicles.

The outstanding example of overconfidence in small calibre anti-tank guns was the use of the little Hotchkiss 25 mm in France, although its muzzle velocity made up for its light weight. Second thoughts led to the study of the Puteaux 47 mm but it was not developed in time.

The British 2-pound anti-tank gun was no better than the French 75 mm. Both were successful only when they could hit tanks square on. They destroyed some German tanks, but too few to stop the massive waves of a tank charge. The final verdict on all fronts, was that this specialised weapon, on which so many hopes had been pinned, was of no use whatever.

Though Anglo-French tank charges in 1940 were mostly on a small-scale, the Germans were to find their 37 mm gun equally inefficient.

The Belgian 47 mm had some spectacular but all too rare successes against German armoured vehicles. For example on 12 May 1940 a single gun which had already seen years of service in artillery school managed to hold off a whole column of the 5th Panzer Division trying to cross the Meuse at Yvoir. With his first shot, Corporal Desnet scored a bull's-eye on a German armoured car; the shell went straight through to hit the vehicle behind.

The Americans had confidence in their 37 mm, and claimed it could pierce $1\frac{1}{2}$ in. of armour at 1,000 yards. They mounted this small gun on fast vehicles to use as a tank-destroyer whose only protection would be its mobility. Fortunately, it was not long before this was seen to be impracticable, and the efficiency of the gun itself questioned, although the 37 mm was used in the Pacific throughout the war with great success against Japanese tanks.

The German 37 mm was less successful against the heavy armour on Russian tanks, revealing a need for heavier guns. From the first the Russians, who had quantities of 45 mm anti-tank guns, realised the need for heavier artillery against German medium tanks.

ANTI-TANK RIFLES

From the above, the reader will not be led to expect much of this category, for these weapons were even lighter. The first anti-tank rifles appeared in the German army in 1918.

The German models were quickly abandoned, but from 1941 onwards Russian troops were issued with quantities of the belatedly but hurriedly produced Degtiarev (PTRD) and the similar Simonov (PTRS). The former, a light anti-tank rifle firing single shots, could pierce 38 mm of armour at 1,000 ft; the latter, a 5-round repeater, was equally powerful over a range of 1,500 ft. Already illustrated in volume 1,[1] we mention them again because they were the only small calibre (14.5 mm) anti-tank weapons used in the whole of the war.

The Russians claim that these simple and rugged rifles were extremely efficient against the first three types of tank, and in 1943 a German

1 Page 87.

SPECIAL ARTILLERY: ROCKET-LAUNCHERS

1. Model BM-8—2. BM-13—3. BM-31. These rocket-launchers, which the Russians nicknamed 'Katiuchas' and the Germans 'Stalin organs' were of 75 mm to 220 mm calibre. They first appeared in the summer of 1941 and were fixed on to various kinds of trucks, such as the Russian Zis-6, or one of the various American makes, Studebaker, Ford, etc., or one of the British trucks given by the Allies under Lend-Lease. All the principal belligerents imitated it. The Americans put it onto their 'Sherman' tanks

4. German 150 mm rocket-launcher named 'Nebelwerfer 41'. The rockets weighed about 88 lbs and were used on a large scale for the first time at Cassino on the Italian front, then in Normandy in 1944. A more powerful version had only five tubes, which fired a 220 mm rocket. The stand with a round base visible between the wheels was lowered for firing. Only one rocket at a time was fired, for to shoot them all simultaneously would have turned the launcher upside-down, but six rounds could be fired in only ten seconds. The man with the helmet is wearing the 1944 model *Feldbluse* jacket with the distinctive marking of the rocket-launching artillery on collar and epaulettes

L. & F. FUNCKEN

technical officer in the army wrote that they were the best of their kind.

279 Degtiarev's and Simonov's were issued per division, but after the battle of Kursk and with the appearance of a new generation of German tanks the number decreased by two-thirds. Some could still be seen in the last days of the battle of Berlin, and no one seeing them fire at pockets of resistance in ruined buildings was left in any doubt as to their efficiency.

But to use this type of weapon against armoured vehicles required courage of a special order. Ludendorff wrote in his memoirs that it was 'a question of courage'. One had to be extraordinarily cool to be able to fire the number of rounds needed to disable a tank's crew while the tank continued to bear down upon one.

THE NEW GENERATION

To make up for the inefficiency of their 37 mm anti-tank gun, of which each division had 72, the Germans used whatever they could lay their hands on, beginning with the excellent French and Belgian 47 mm guns. Ever since the 1914–18 war German artillery schools had preached the use of anti-aircraft guns against fast-moving armoured vehicles, and now this lesson was put into practice. In Russia German anti-aircraft units of all calibres frequently destroyed more tanks than planes.

Luckily for them, the Russians had an excellent 45 mm gun which could stop light and medium enemy tanks. It was quickly backed up with a rapid-fire 37 mm anti-aircraft gun as a stopgap while awaiting the arrival of a long-barrelled high muzzle-velocity 45 mm gun known as the model 42. The following spring, the struggle between armour-plating and calibre took another turn, with the appearance of a 1943 model 55 mm SIS 2. But the most famous of all Russian anti-tank guns was without doubt the 1942 76.2 mm SIS 3 which put paid to hundreds of medium tanks at Moscow, Stalingrad and Kursk, and was used right up until Berlin.

The British and the Americans were not so fortunate. They could not afford to use an intermediary weapon while they developed a more powerful gun. In Libya the British had to face Germany's might with the 6-pounder on its 2-spread gun-carriage. This had a relatively rapid rate of fire, but still far less than that of the German 88 mm gun which opposed it. Judging by British and American experience, traditional artillery was most unsatisfactory as an anti-tank device.

In 1941 the Germans began using their first long-barrelled recoilless anti-tank gun – the PzB 41 28 mm. Invented in 1890 by de Place, a French captain, the breech-brake allowed some of the gases created by the explosion to escape through lateral holes, thus counteracting the tendency to recoil. It had hardly been used before the Second World War.

Though the 28 mm gun's ammunition was small, its high muzzle-velocity enabled it to pierce 2 in. of armour at 440 yds. Nonetheless it was largely outclassed by the Pak 38 (*Panzerabwehrkanone* 38) of 50 mm calibre, whose 57 mm shells had twice the power of penetration of the English 6-pounder.

In 1942 this weapon was the standard armament for German anti-tank units, and proved deadly. Sunk 1 ft into the sand and carefully camouflaged, its silhouette was so low and difficult to spot that it was usually the first to strike.

The terrible 88 or Pak 43, mounted on a cruciform gun-carriage, was less than 4 ft high, making it easy to camouflage and presenting a very small target even at close range.

For the Germans, the greatest threat was the way their enemies, both Russian and American, produced vast numbers of armoured vehicles; for this reason they needed first-class anti-tank weapons. Apart from those mentioned above,

TRADITIONAL ANTI-TANK ARTILLERY

1. British 2-pounder (30 mm) gun—2. Belgian 47 mm gun—3. American 37 mm gun—4. Russian 45 mm model 42—5. British 6-pounder (57 mm) gun—6. German Pak-41 42/28 mm—7. French 25 mm—8. German 50 mm Pak 38—9. German 88 mm Pak 43 in normal firing position—10. 88 mm Pak 43 on its trailer. It could also be fired in this position

there were also the Pak 43/41 (88 mm) and the Pak 41 (75 mm).

One should not forget the use of captured enemy weapons. For example there was the 47 mm Czechoslovak Pak Skoda (soon outdated), the 75 mm Pak 97/38 made in 1942 from French 75s (mounted on a Pak 38 gun-carriage and recognisable by its metal wheels, the metal wheel discs arranged in tricycle formation with the third wheel placed at the end of the trailer), and finally the Pak 36 and the FK (*Feldkanone*) 39, both 76.2 mm and of Russian origin.

First seen in Sicily in 1943, the FK 39 was basically the same as the Russian model 1939 field gun. The barrel was shorter now, had a breech brake, and was modified for Pak 36 ammunition. Far more famous was the 76.2 mm Pak 36, an adaptation of the Russian 297 sometimes called the Pulitov. Thousands were captured in the first battles on the Russian front, and they made their mark in Libya for the first time in March 1942 with their astonishing accuracy. Only when the Germans retreated a few weeks later were they identified. They were very useful at Gazala and El Alamein, backing up the 88s which had become scarce.

German anti-tank superiority was due not only to the quality and quantity of her guns, but also largely to her ammunition, whose powers of penetration and ballistic qualities were never equalled by the Allies.

The Hollow Charge

In 1890 an American scientist, C. E. Munroe, published the results of one of his experiments, in which he had used explosives to engrave on a sheet of metal. To demonstrate his discovery, this scientist had carved his name in mirror writing on a block of explosives. He then put the explosives against a thick sheet of metal, and when he detonated it, his name was engraved on the sheet.

This phenomenon, the 'Munroe effect', was patented in Britain and Germany as a means of engraving metal and then forgotten. Only the metal plaque remained, displayed under glass in the Philadelphia Museum of Technology.

If by chance Munroe had used more explosives or a thinner metal plate the metal would have been completely cut away, and the principle of hollow-charge explosives would have been discovered accidentally fifty years sooner.

Prior to making this minor experiment, Munroe had tried his technique on the door of an old safe – some 5 in. of solid steel. He made up a bundle of sticks of dynamite in such a way that the centre formed a cone-shaped hollow. Placing this against the steel and detonating it, Munroe found he had made a 3 in. deep hole, but when he used an equivalent charge of dynamite without the cone-shaped hollow, it had almost no effect.

It was found that the cause of this newly discovered phenomenon lay in the extraordinary power of the shock-wave, which fired a thin dart or jet of flame at a speed of five or six miles per second. Subsequently it was found that if one lined the cavity of the charge with a metal skin, the penetrating power was increased by the bombardment of metal particles.

The first time Munroe's discovery was used for military purposes was in France. Just before the war, an anti-tank grenade that could be fired from a rifle had been perfected, whose manufacture was prevented only by the German invasion of the whole of France in 1942. At the same time, the United States was trying to use the Munroe effect for rocket and artillery shells.

From the start hollow-charge projectiles were provided with a conical lid to cover the hollow crater in the explosive charge. It must be stressed that this thin metal sheet, whatever its shape and dimensions, served only as a cover to facilitate handling, protect the explosive and give it better aerodynamics. On contact with the target, this nose-cone reinforced the effect of the explosion as explained above, and furthermore its impact acted on a simple inertia-hammer which hit a percussion cap and detonator. This was all situated at the far end of the shell behind the explosive.

It is interesting to learn that in the light of some experiments, one can see that this core of metal particles did not always pierce the armour itself. Sometimes the combination of air and gas alone behaved like an armour-piercing projectile.

Unlikely as it may seem, this strange phenomenon is similar to that of fluid under pressure attacking the hardest rocks. In our case, the gas created an explosion equivalent to a muzzle velocity of 30,000 feet per second in the case of the bazooka or British P.I.A.T. shells.

It should also be noted that the relatively small interior of the tank hit would be filled with flying shrapnel.

The penetrating power of these appalling projectiles varied, of course, according to their size.

HOLLOW-CHARGE WEAPONS

The smallest of these were the hand-grenades and grenades fired by rifle, and most of these were German. In spite of their small size and despite charges weighing only between 3 and 10 oz, the German anti-tank grenades fired by traditional rifles with wooden ball cartridges or grenade-launchers could penetrate armour between 2½ and 5 inches thick at a range of 100 to 200 yds.

The strangest use of hollow-charge arms in the infantry was the German *Panzerwurfmine* – an anti-tank grenade with a handle thrown from a range of 20 or 30 yds which was automatically primed by the opening of a little parachute.

Since bazookas, *Panzerschrecks* and *Panzerfausts* have been mentioned in the chapters on the American and German armies, we shall mention here some of the other weapons in this enormous family.

The unpopular British Boys[1] anti-tank rifle was finally replaced by the P.I.A.T. or 'Projector, Infantry, Anti-tank'. Despite its bizarre appearance something between an anti-tank rifle and a bazooka, the P.I.A.T. was certainly one of the finest weapons of its kind. Weighing only about 31 lb, it could be carried by one man and was fired from the shoulder like a rifle although it had

quite a kick! In Italy a soldier caught up in the heat of battle took aim at an enemy tank and fired standing up rather than from the recommended position lying flat. So severe was the kick, that he was thrown 10 ft back ... the tank was destroyed nevertheless.

One of the P.I.A.T.'s major defects was its relatively short range. It could pierce 4 in.-thick armour at 100 yds, that is to say at half the range of its German and American equivalents. Another defect was the fact that its shells deteriorated if kept too long. So great was the risk of accidental explosion that the P.I.A.T.s were not used in manoeuvres after the war.

Nevertheless this strange weapon was widely used and parachuted to the French Resistance, where it was one of their major weapons. The P.I.A.T. also had the advantage of being able to fire conventional shells such as mortar rounds at a range of more than 650 yds.

The Japanese never got beyond the use of the simplest hollow-charge shells. Three types of funnel-shaped hand-grenade were made with a wooden base, silk outer covering and adorned with a bunch of long hempen hairs to give stability. It was claimed to be able to pierce 3 in. of armour.

An even more primitive device was used in the units specialising in hand-to-hand fighting. It consisted of a cone of sheet steel on the end of a 6-ft pole. Three long nails were fixed around the base of the cone so that if the charge were placed against enemy armour it would be at the optimum distance for deepest penetration, i.e. about 6 in. The Japanese soldier then had to push on the end of the pole to press a detonator in the charge and set it off. Under 'ideal conditions' it was possible to penetrate 6 in. armour, and 4 in. at an angle of 60°. It is not known what effect this infernal device had on its operator!

The Russians do not seem to have developed any weapon of this kind. They were quite happy with the bazookas they got from America under Lend-Lease, though there is no photographic

1 See volume 2 of this series, pages 14–15.

evidence of this. No doubt the Russians also used German hollow-charge weapons when they fell into their hands.

In the field of traditional artillery, the Germans thought they could improve their 37 mm anti-tank gun by making it fire a new kind of shell which could take care of the increasing thickness of Russian armour-plating. These hollow-charge shells could get through 6 in. of steel at 200 yds. Old French 75 mm guns were converted to take this new ammunition and become anti-tank guns.

In America research into increasing the bazooka's range spread into traditional artillery methods. Working in the greatest secrecy, America finally developed a standardised 105 mm round which made a promising first appearance in North Africa.

HOLLOW-CHARGE ANTI-TANK ARTILLERY

1. 190 mm Japanese type 10 rocket-launcher. At the foot of the ramp one can see the charge and the bomb itself, weighing some 130 lbs. Its range could be adjusted by modifying the angle of the ramp, using a system of hooks. Ignition was by remote control—2. Japanese hollow-charge with handle—3. Japanese hollow-charge grenade. There were three versions: 3 lbs, 4 lbs and 6 lbs—4. 88 mm *Raketenwerfer* 43, nicknamed 'Püppchen' (Little Doll). Its 'tyres' are made of light metal on shock-absorbers; obviously, this gun was not meant to move long distances on its own wheels—5. German 37 mm gun coverted for firing hollow-charge rounds—6. German parachutists' recoilless gun, 105 mm

1

2

3

4

5

6

MILITARY TRANSPORT VEHICLES

The United States

In the previous volume we mentioned how some of the fighting countries had a wide range of transport vehicles, but none could compare with the fantastic number of vehicles produced in the USA.

Without any doubt, the most famous by far was the Jeep, a small all-purpose vehicle. An engineer named Karl Probst made the first sketches in 1940; vehicles were tested, improved and redesigned by three different firms simultaneously: Bantam, Willys and Ford.

The three types of jeep that were built had to go through all kinds of tests, under the close scrutiny of army observers. In the end, they chose the Willys, and after a few minor changes, mass production began at Willys at the end of 1941 and at Ford at the beginning of 1942. It was called the GPW or 'General Purpose Willys', but very soon it acquired nicknames such as the 'Peep', 'Blitz Buggy' and finally the 'Jeep' (short for GP).

This splendid little car lived up to its name, managing to carry out an extraordinary number of jobs on all fronts with considerable dash. Sometimes GIs transformed it into a little armoured car by improvising an armour from steel sheets. They even managed to make it into a fake 'Kübelwagen' with a dummy chauffeur in a steel helmet to fool the Afrika Korps' sentries. In all, some 640,000 Jeeps were built.

As for trucks, there were dozens of different kinds of Fords, Chevrolets, G.M.C.s, Dodges, etc. All told, there were some 990,000 light vehicles, 800,000 medium and 580,000 heavy vehicles, making a grand total of something like 3,300,000 transport vehicles.

Russia

Industry in Russia tended to concentrate on the large armoured vehicles which she needed most urgently. As a result, there were fewer indigenous transport vehicles than in the United States, and only a few different models.

Under Lend-Lease agreement, Russia received 51,500 jeeps, 35,000 motorbikes, 375,000 trucks and 8,000 tractors, to say nothing of 1,900 locomotives and 189,000 field telephones. Nonetheless Russian historians consider that Allied aid had only a minor role to play in the liberation of Russia.

Japan

The Japanese automobile industry was very young and, in comparison with the other major powers, produced very few military transport vehicles. In 1941 production peaked at 30,000, falling to less than 7,000 in 1945 when all effort was concentrated on building planes.

TRANSPORTS

1. British Fordson. There were a number of different trucks of this type made by Morris, Bedford, etc.—2. Jeep—3. American GMC truck. At the time of the landings in Europe, all Allied vehicles had to display a white star in a white circle so that Allied planes would recognise them—4. Japanese car—5. Russian jeep

6. Junkers 52, German parachutists' 'Aunty Ju'. A bomber during the Spanish Civil War, it was given a new lease of life in all the campaigns from 1939 to 1945—7. The most famous of all transporter planes, the Douglas C-53 'Sky-trooper' troop-transporter, also known as the Douglas C-47 'Skytrain' in its guise as freighter, but best known under its British nickname, 'Dakota'. It was a military version of the DC-3.

1

2

3

6

7

4

5

L. & F. Funcken

PART FOUR

SUBMARINES, SHIPPING AND AIRCRAFT

SUBMARINES

It was only when submarines adopted diesel motors, periscopes and gyro-compasses during the 1914–18 war that they became a serious threat. Maritime law had tried to regulate their use: well before 1914 it was generally accepted that no nation should sink an enemy's merchant ship without having first looked after its crew's safety, by putting out lifeboats or by taking the men aboard. But it goes without saying that though this was no problem for surface vessels, it was extremely restricting for a submarine which could be sunk by any moderately skilled gunner while waiting for lifeboats to be launched. Germany claimed that the Allies had violated the laws of naval warfare in this way, and used this as an excuse for sinking any enemy ship on sight in reprisal.

After the war, the Washington Disarmament Conference confirmed the previous protocol, and this was repeated in the 1936 London protocol, signed by all those who were to fight later in the Second World War. Once more the same misunderstandings occurred, and little by little war at sea developed into total war.

The results were appalling. U-boats sank 29 American and 158 British warships, but the Allied merchant fleet's total loss reached the amazing figure of 23,251,000 tons. During the war, the Germans built 1,100 submarines of at least twenty different kinds, but when war broke out there were only thirty or so able to carry out a long mission.

It is often thought that submarines operated, as their name implies, under water for most of the time; in fact submarines were primarily surface vessels able to dive, going underwater only in order to escape being spotted by the enemy, or when preparing to attack.

Under water, their performance was drastically reduced since they now had to run off electric instead of their powerful diesel motors, which would have used up too much precious oxygen. At top speed, a submarine could stay under water for an hour only; going slower, it could stay submerged for between 12 and 24 hours depending on its category. Sooner or later, U-boats had to surface, whether they liked it or not, to recharge their batteries by running their diesel motors.

Thus aeroplanes became a considerable nuisance, for there was always the danger of their

AMERICAN NAVY I

1. Officer in winter full-dress uniform. In summer the cap was white—2. Summer undress—3. Ensign 1st class, a pilot in the naval air force, in winter working-dress uniform—4. Caps of Admirals, Vice-Admirals, Rear Admirals and Commodores—5. Commander and Captain—6. Other officers—7. Summer cap. Cap badges: 8. Metal—9. Embroidered—10. Embroidered, but of rather unusual appearance here, although it is copied from that worn by Admiral Mark A. Mitscher, one of the most popular characters in the US Navy

Badges of rank (worn on shirt collar in summer undress): 11. Ship's ensign 2nd class—12. Ship's ensign 1st class—13. Lieutenant—14. Lieutenant-Commander—15. Commander—16. Captain—17. Commodore—18. Rear Admiral—19. Vice-Admiral—20. Admiral (or Vice-Admiral with rank of Commander-in-Chief)

Epaulettes (for winter and summer dress): 21. Ship's ensign 2nd class—22. Ship's ensign 1st class—23. Lieutenant—24. Lieutenant-Commander—25. Commander—26. Captain—27. Commodore—28. Rear Admiral—29. Vice-Admiral—30. Admiral—31–40. Ranks worn on the sleeves (in the same order as the above)

Service badges: 41. Dentist—42. Health—43. Provisions—44. Engineers—These badges replaced the general service star shown in figs 21–40. Badges worn on the chest: 45. Pilot (see fig. 3)—46. Observer—47. Naval air force doctor—48. Balloon pilot—49. Submarine doctor—50. Submarine officer

appearing when the submarine had to come up for air. To parry this threat, more anti-aircraft guns were used, then radar. But the third, and by far the most efficient, defence measure was the snorkel, which allowed diesel engines to be used under water by breathing air sucked in from above.

The Germans tried to make a 'real' submarine using the Walter hydrogen peroxide motor, but it was too late.

The three leading submarine captains, Prien, Kretschner, and Schepke sank some 800,000 tons of Allied shipping between them. They were brought together in March 1941 to attack an important convoy but disappeared at eight-day intervals. All told, of the 39,000 men who served in Admiral Dönitz's U-boat packs, 32,000 officers and men disappeared.

Here follows a list of losses on both sides of this appalling underwater war:

	GERMAN U-BOATS SUNK:	ALLIED SHIPPING SUNK:
1939 (Sept.–Dec.)	9	810,000 tons
1940	22	4,407,000 tons
1941	35	4,398,000 tons
1942	85	8,245,000 tons
1943	237	3,616,000 tons
1944	241	1,422,000 tons
1945 (Jan.–May)	153	458,000 tons

On the Allied side, American submarines were extremely effective against Japanese merchant ships, sinking 1,150 of them for 52 submarines lost. The British operating mainly in the Mediterranean, were outstandingly courageous. The *Upholder* alone sank 97,000 tons of enemy shipping.

AMERICAN NAVY II

1. Winter service dress—2. Summer service dress with braiding indicating four years' service—3. Cadet sailor—4. Sailor without special trade—5. Sailor, graduate of staff college—6. Quartermaster—7. Quartermaster 1st class—8. 2nd class petty officer—9. Petty officer. All wear the badge showing their speciality between the eagle and the chevron. Badges showing a special trade: 10. Radio station operator—11. Gun-layer—12. Boatswain—13. Gunner—14. Signaller—15. Radio

Badges of senior petty officers: 16. 1st petty officer—17. Chief petty officer. Superior petty officers wore on their epaulettes and sleeves badges showing their special trade; likewise on

Miniature Submarines

Many countries used small submarines with varying degrees of success. The Germans had the largest number of different kinds, ranging from 16 tons to single-seater human torpedoes. They were used on the Meuse and Scheldt estuaries as well as along the Channel coast and are credited with two cargo ships and 90,000 tons of light shipping in the months that followed the invasion.

After Pearl Harbor onwards, the Japanese made extensive use of miniature submarines but sank only one small ship.

The Italians were much more skilful and luckier with their SLC (*Siluro a Lenta Corsa*) human torpedoes, which were remarkably successful in Crete, Gibraltar, and particularly Alexandria, where they put the battleships *Queen Elizabeth* and *Valiant* out of action for a long period.

The British, for their part, built a whole fleet of midget submarines. One of them, the X-7, managed to inflict some damage on the *Tirpitz* when she was moored in Norway. The Japanese cruiser *Tokao* was destroyed by these craft in Singapore harbour.

the collar of their khaki shirt when worn (working dress). Chief officers had gilt badges (figs 18–26); 1st officers had identical badges in silver—18. Meteorologist—19. Photographer—20. Chemist—21. Gunner—22. Radio—23. Carpenter—24. Mechanic—25. Electrician—26. Paymaster

27. 1st officer. On his collar and shoulders he would be wearing one of the above badges—28. Officer with chevrons of rank as in fig. 9, which are in yellow here to go with blue uniforms—29. Officers' cap badge—30. 1st officers' cap badge—31. Landing section leader with Reising model 55, 45 calibre sub-machine-gun (11.43 mm) with folding butt, mostly issued to sailors and Home-Guard units—32. Sailor in one-piece battledress. These two men are not marines

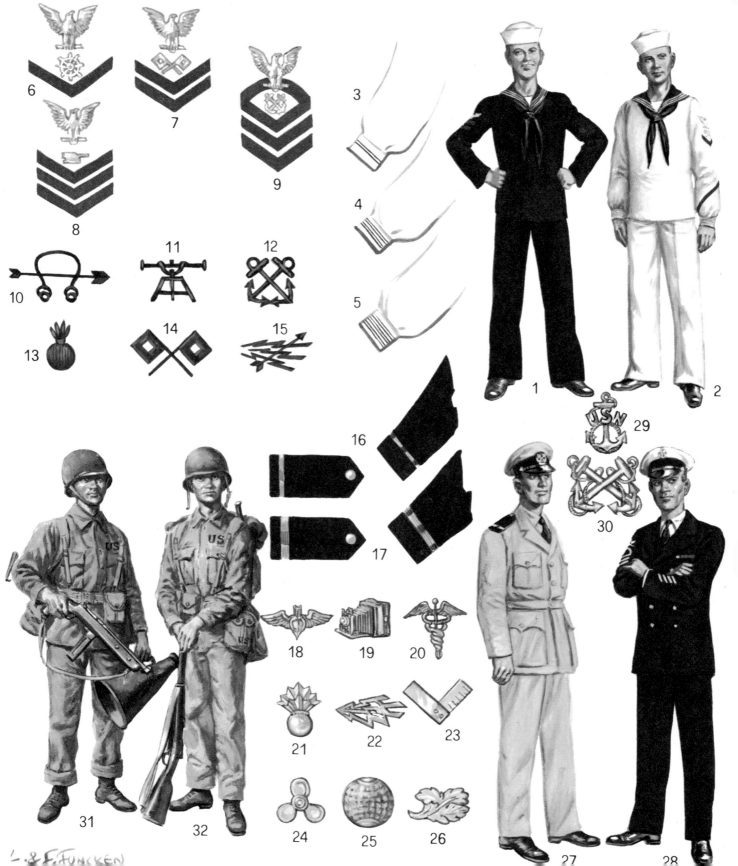

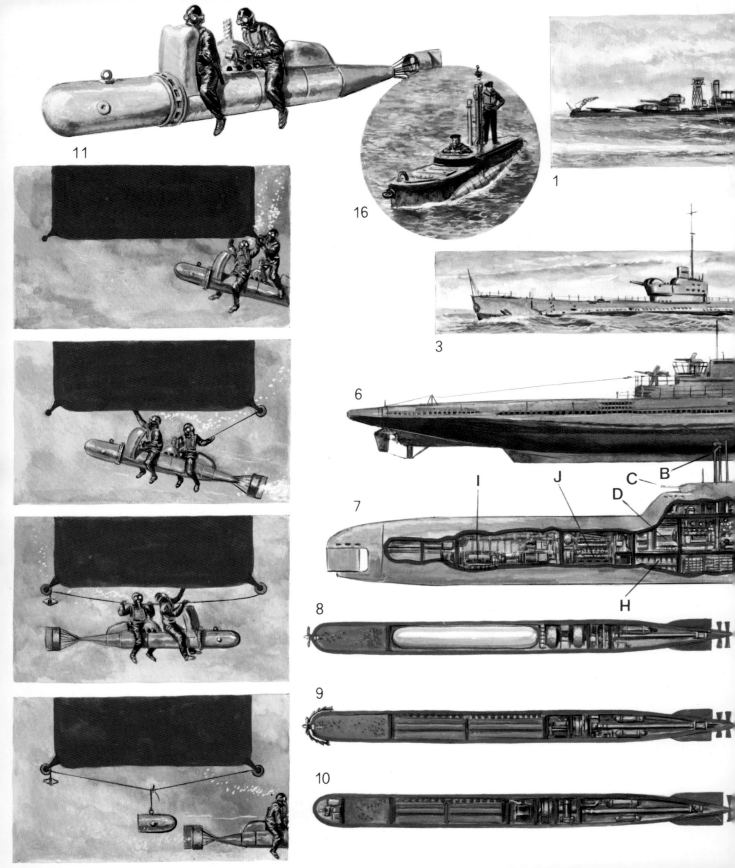

11

16

1

3

6

7

I

J

B

C

D

H

8

9

10

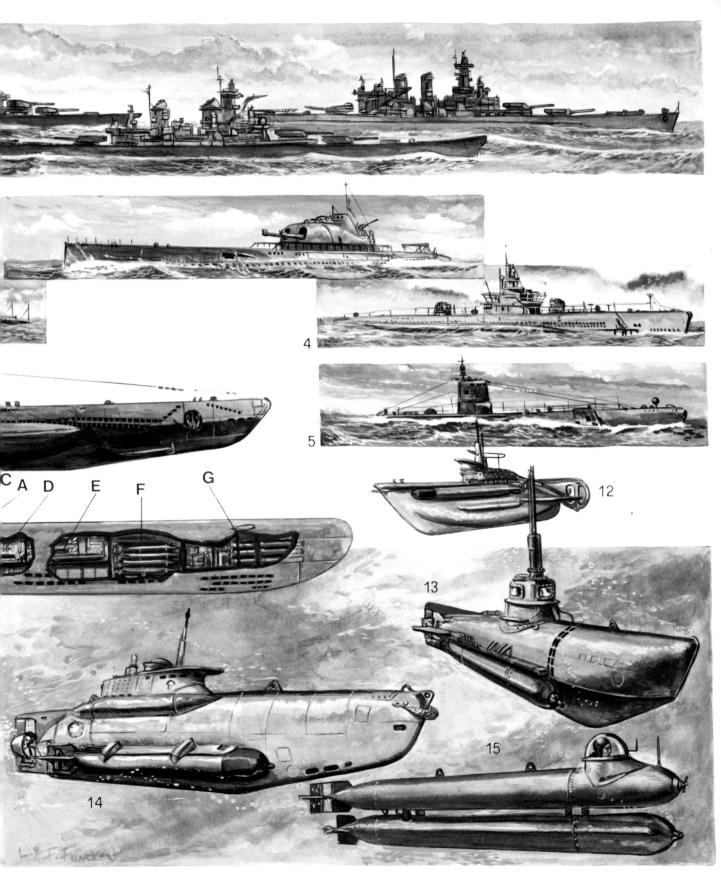

4

5

C A D E F G

12

13

14

15

L. & F. FUNCKEN

THE NAVY AND NAVAL AIR ARMS

The US Navy

It was only after the Civil War of 1861–5 that America first realised the importance of a navy, for during the war both the South and the North used warships to threaten harbours and coastline. Incidentally, it was during the Civil War that the first fight between two iron-clad battleships took place.

By the end of the war, the United States fleet consisted of about forty ships. When the Cuban colonies revolted and the American battleship *Maine* blew up in Havana, the Spanish-American war broke out and the fleet was increased. The dawning of the 20th century saw the US navy far weaker still than that of other great nations. But it made huge strides under President Theodore Roosevelt, and thanks to a budget which increased to 361 million dollars in 1904 and to 725 million dollars in 1910. On the eve of the First World War the US navy ranked third, behind Germany and

SHIPS AND SUBMARINES (pages 96–7)

1. American Navy. From left to right: the *Colorado* (note the towers typical of old-style American warships); the *Iowa*, the most powerful ship in the Navy; the *North Carolina*, one of the first two new ships to be commissioned after 1941—2. The French submarine *Surcouf*, the largest in the world at the time. It was sunk in 1942—3. British 'P Class' submarine (P for Parthian)—4. Submarine *Archerfish* (American)—5. Italian submarine, *Giada*—6. German U-boat (*Unterseeboot* = submarine), type VIIC, the most commonly used. 44 crew and 225 ft long—7. U-boat type XXIC: A. Command post; B. Snorkel; C. Four 30 mm guns; D. Officers' mess; E. Crew's quarters; F. Torpedo room; G. Six torpedo tubes; H. Batteries; I. Electric motors; J. Diesel motors

Torpedos: 8. Silent, compressed air (wake of bubbles)—9. With electric motor (bubbles suppressed)—10. Electrically driven and with acoustic control. The little propellor on the front visible in 8 and 9 was used to prime the explosive after the torpedo had travelled a certain distance; this prevented premature explosions

11. *Siluro a lenta corsa*, also known as the 'Maiale' (Pig), an Italian human torpedo with removable head. Underneath one can see the various laborious stages necessary for suspending the charge from a steel cable previously attached to the enemy ship's stabilisers—12. The Italian pocket submarine *Costiero*—German pocket submarines: 13. 'Biber' (Beaver). Crew of one, length 40 ft—14. 'Seehund' (Seadog). Crew of two, length 26 ft—15. Human torpedo 'Neger' (Negro). Crew of one, length 27 ft. It travelled with its dome above the surface; the pilot wore a wetsuit so that he could swim to shore if the transporter broke down after the torpedo had been launched—16. 'Midget', British pocket submarine. Crew of four, length 66 ft . All these miniature submarines were very difficult to handle; with the possible exception of the 'Seehund', they were nothing less than death-traps for their intrepid crews

AMERICAN NAVY, MARINE CORPS

1. A non-commissioned officer (Sergeant, chief of section) in full-dress uniform—2. Sergeant in winter service dress—3. Officer in full-dress uniform—4. Officer in winter dress. His uniform's dark-green colour is similar to that of the old light infantry corps' uniform

Ranks: 5. Soldier, 1st class—6. Corporal—7. Sergeant—8. Administration Sergeant—9. Sergeant, chief of section—10. Technician Sergeant—11. Major—12. Technician staff Sergeant—13. Sergeant-Major. On summer uniforms and light-khaki or dark-green field service dress, these chevrons were dark blue on an olive-green ground—14. Lieutenant-General—15. Major-General—16. Brigadier—17. Colonel—18. Lieutenant-Colonel—19. Major—20. Captain—21. Lieutenant—22. Sub-Lieutenant—23. Sergeant-Major—24. Adjutant

25. Officers' cap. They alone could wear the Hungarian knot—26. Cap badges for officers and (above right) soldiers. Badges visible between figs 1 and 2 and between figs 3 and 4 are collar badges worn on the right side—27. Combat uniform, camouflaged—28. The fatigue dress that the marines preferred for battledress. Marines were issued with the latest arms including the M1 carbine, the Garand M1 rifle and the M3 sub-machine-gun. The Marine in fig. 28 has a Johnson M.1941 7.62 mm semi-automatic rifle with 10 rounds

Arm badges of Marines and some of the other units who fought in the Pacific: 29. 45th Division. They relieved the Marines in the Willaumez peninsular—30. 1st Marine Amphibious Corps with Rangers' death-head. Parachutists had an open parachute instead, flight engineers a winged, fortified castle, etc.—31. 3rd Marine Division—32. 4th Division—33. 5th Amphibious Corps—34. 1st Cavalry Division

5

6

7

8

9

10

11

12

13

2

29

30

31

32

33

27

28

14

15

16

17

18

1

2

23

25

34

3

4

24

26

L. & F. Fun...

Great Britain, who was first. This troubled America, and when Britain was in a critical financial position at the end of the war, America managed to persuade her to abandon the 'two power standard' which gave the Royal Navy the right to a fleet as big as those of the two other major powers put together. This transition from the two power standard to a one power standard brought the American navy up to the level of its ally.

The completion of the Panama Canal in 1914 was a major step forward for the United States, which was now no longer obliged to keep two separate fleets, one in the Pacific and one in the Atlantic. If the fleets had to be combined, their distance apart was much shorter now that it was no longer necessary to go round Cape Horn. One can understand from this how important the Panama Canal remains for the security of the United States.

In 1939 the American fleet was composed as follows:

Battleships	15 (8)
Heavy cruisers	18
Light cruisers	17 (2)
Aircraft carriers	5 (1)
Destroyers	215 (19)
Submarines	87
Torpedo boats	— (13)

NB: Figures in brackets refer to ships under construction.

When the Japanese attacked, the Pacific fleet consisted of 9 battleships, 13 heavy cruisers, 11 light cruisers, 3 aircraft carriers, 80 destroyers and 56 submarines. It should be stressed that to divide the American fleet into two halves is an oversimplification since in 1940 there were several fleets – the battle force, the scout force, the Atlantic force and an Asiatic force. There was a base force with a separate command structure and a submarine force which came under the battle force.

After the catastrophe at Pearl Harbor, America was remarkably quick at pulling herself together, building a total of 8,200,000 tons of warships – 8 battleships, 13 heavy cruisers, 2 battle cruisers, 33 light cruisers, 18 large aircraft carriers, 9 small

aircraft carriers, 110 escort aircraft carriers, 352 destroyers, 12 mine-layers, 498 escort destroyers, 55 rapid transport ships, 203 submarines and more than 100,000 patrol-boats, launches and landing ships – an enormous armada with a mass of radar and ultrasonic devices which increased its power tenfold.

By the end of 1940 it was 120,000 volunteers strong; by the end of 1941 there were 175,000 sailors and 12,000 officers. By the end of the war the US navy had 800,000 men and was the most powerful navy in the world. 72,554 men were lost.

THE US NAVY AT WAR

On 1, 6 and 7 June 1942 Pearl Harbor was avenged at Midway. It was Japan's first naval defeat since 1592, for against American losses of 150 planes, 1 aircraft carrier and 1 cruiser, the Japanese lost 275 planes and 3 aircraft carriers. Over the following years, the American navy fought a long series of battles to reconquer the Pacific, in particular in 1944 at the second and decisive battle of the Philippines. Between 23 and 25 October, 12 battleships, 34 aircraft carriers, 23 cruisers and 118 destroyers crushed a smaller Japanese fleet which had 4 aircraft carriers (whose 116 planes were no match for the 1,280 enemy

AMERICAN NAVY, COASTGUARDS AND NURSES

1. Coastguard sailor; on the left shoulder he has a machine-operator's braiding. The same braiding in blue, worn on the right shoulder, denotes an ordinary sailor—2. Naval nurse in 1929–1941 uniform—3. Naval nurse in 1943 uniform. The austere pre-war uniform changed slowly to follow civilian fashions—4. Coastguard officer. Apart from the shield on the sleeve, the uniform, badges and braiding were exactly the same as those in the Marines—5. Officer in summer dress. Apart from the shield, the epaulette (detail on the right) was similar to that in the Navy—6. Quartermaster with boatswain's badge—7. Officer—8. 1st petty officer—9. Ensign—10. Shore-based personnel's cap. *Cap badges:* 11. Shore-based personnel—12. 1st petty officer—13. Petty officer—14. Officer and chief petty officer—15. Sleeve badges for officer or first mate. The same badge in silver was for petty officers; it was blue for other ranks

16. Navy Nurse Corps badge—17. Official headgear in 1944 with usual badge. Summer dress—18. Ditto, winter dress—19. The NNC badge was moved down to the sleeves at the same time as the new headgear was issued—20. The unit badge was worn on the left of the field service cap and the rank shown on the right

6

7

8

9

10

11

12

13

14

15

16

1

2

3

4

5

17

18

19

20

planes), 7 battleships, 22 cruisers and 35 destroyers. The game was up: 26 Japanese ships were sunk for only 6 American.

THE MARINES

The war in the Pacific gave the US Marine Corps a special place in military history. It had always been made up of volunteers, ever since the first two battalions were formed in 1775 as landing parties for the new navy. They first saw active combat in the Bahamas in 1776, and from that date, the Marines have taken part in all America's wars.

The 'Leathernecks'' claim to fame (this name derives from the leather rear peak of helmets worn in the 18th century) must be in the 300 landings in which they took part.

18,000 men strong in 1921, the Corps soon began to acquire those qualities which were to make it such a powerful tool in amphibious warfare. Its final complement was 669,100 men, of whom approximately 450,000 saw active service and 24,551 were killed.

The Marines' most bloody battles took place between 19 February and 26 March 1945 with the capture of the island of Iwo Jima.

It was in the southern Pacific that the Marines first used the most unorthodox (but highly effective) way of getting round the fact that the Japanese were listening in to their radio transmissions. A contingent of Navaho Indians in the radio units spoke clearly in their own language, without bothering to encode and decode their messages, for the Japanese, quite understandably, had no Navaho interpreters!

COAST GUARDS

A few small ships armed with guns and tracking smugglers were the humble origins of the American coastguards in the 1790s. In 1915 the Rescue Service was added, followed by the Lighthouse Service in 1939. In that same year the coastguards were taken into the American armed forces for the duration of hostilities. But the coastguards had been active long before then – it is said that the coastguards made the first capture of an enemy vessel in the War of 1812.

During the First World War, coastguards hunted submarines and escorted convoys between Gibraltar and Great Britain.

In 1941 the work and numbers of coastguards were increased considerably, so that 170,000 men and 800 ships took part in the anti-submarine war, scoring 11 'kills'; thousands of shipwrecked sailors were rescued, but their most valiant exploit, although paradoxically the least known, was during the invasion, when coastguards provided the pilots for ships for the landings in Africa, Europe and the Pacific. They were indefatigable, and many a GI floundering in front of the Normandy beaches was saved by coastguards who had experience of small boats. 572 men were killed, fighting under their motto *Semper paratus* ('Always Ready').

LANDING CRAFT

In preceding wars and especially in the Dardanelles in 1915, combined operations and landings had been catastrophic. The Allies were faced with many problems in having to invade Europe. Fortunately, American experts were determined to solve the problem and came up with an enormous fleet of eighty different kinds of ship, from inflatable rafts to LSD (Dock Landing Ship) which weighed more than 10,000 tons. Here is a list of the main types of craft used: LCC – Control Landing Craft, LCI – Infantry Landing Craft, LCT – Tank Landing Craft, LCM – Mechanised Equipment Landing Craft, LCV – Vehicle Landing Craft, LCS – Support

LANDING CRAFT AND ARMOURED VEHICLES

1. LCT (Landing Craft Tank)—2. LCI (Landing Craft Infantry)—3. LCA (Landing Craft Assault). The pilots shown here are British—4. LVT (Landing Vehicle Tracked) 'Water Buffalo'. There were several versions of this, of which one had 75 mm howitzer in its turret—5. American light armoured car, the M8, called 'Greyhound' in Great Britain. Widely used in Europe from 1944–45—6. Russian BA 64 armoured car, built in large numbers from 1943

Landing Craft, LCP – Personnel Landing Craft, LCR – Rubber Landing Craft (an inflatable canoe), LSD – Dock Landing Ship, LST – Tank Landing Ship.

Naval Air Power

The battle of Midway was the US naval airforce's first great victory, when they beat the Japanese fleet as they set about annihilating what was left of the American navy and capturing the little island in the Pacific which gave the battle its name.

American planes were based on Midway, and when their Brewster Buffalos, Grummun Avengers and Dauntless first met the Japanese fighters on 4 June 1942 things looked bad: the Zeros were far more powerful and easily destroyed more than half the American planes. Only 8 of the 16 Dauntless from the Marine Corps came back, and 6 of those had been so badly damaged that they would never fly again. Things were even worse, when of the 116 planes that took off from the aircraft carriers *Midway*, *Hornet*, *Enterprise* and *Yorktown*, only half found the enemy without managing to do any damage. Only 12 survived a vicious dogfight, but while the Japanese fleet was advancing intact and unperturbed towards its objective, a squadron of 33 Douglas SBD Dauntless commanded by Lt-Commander MacClusky and belonging to the *Enterprise* appeared. Diving from 3,000 ft at an angle of 70 degrees, the light dive bombers took aim on the *Akagi* and *Kaga* aircraft carriers, which immediately caught fire. Simultaneously, another group of bombers from the *Yorktown* attacked and hit a third aircraft carrier, the *Soryu*, which sank after three torpedoes from the submarine *Nautilus* hit it.

MacClusky was fortunate. In the same afternoon, leading a group of four planes without fighter escort, he attacked the fourth Japanese aircraft carrier, the *Hiryu*. Since the morning this ship had survived a number of attacks, dodging hundreds of bombs and torpedoes, but was now hit four times and sank the next morning. Japanese torpedo boats picked up hundreds of seamen.

With his fleet decimated, the Japanese Admiral gave the order to disengage. Despite numerical inferiority, the Americans had chance on their side, as well as a most daring Admiral, William Nimitz, who was absolutely determined to strike the heaviest possible blow to his enemy. The Japanese were over-confident, and doubted the Americans' fighting potential.

Naval air power continued to grow in importance and to break all the established rules of war at sea.

The battle of Leyte, also known as the second battle of the Philippines, took place from 23 to 28 October 1944. Pushed back little by little by a series of stunning American successes, the Japanese fleet was now based at home and round Singapore. The American landings on the Philippine islands threatened to cut off all the Japanese troops stationed in the South Sea Islands area, as had already happened when the Marianas and Bonin islands were taken. Almost all the Japanese fleet was sent in to attack the bridgehead. 26 ships were lost: 3 battleships, 4 aircraft carriers and 10 cruisers; a dozen more important ships were severely damaged and only 6 battleships, 4 heavy cruisers, 1 light cruiser and 10 destroyers managed to escape in spite of being hit. The American navy had lost only 3 aircraft carriers – 1 medium and 2 light – and 3 destroyers.

Air power played the major part in this victory. Of the losses that the the three Japanese squadrons suffered, three aircraft carriers had been sunk by planes alone, and most of the other ships had been hit or sunk by combined air-sea actions.

BRITISH AND AMERICAN NAVAL AVIATION

1. Fairey Barracuda (1943). It was planes of this purely British type which harassed the *Tirpitz*, leading to its eventual destruction. It was the Royal Navy's first single-winged torpedo plane—2. Fairey Firefly (1943). A photo-reconnaissance version of this fighter spotted the *Tirpitz*. The Firefly flew mainly over the Pacific—3. Supermarine Seafire Mark 1B, the first version of the Spitfire which the Fleet Air Arm adopted in 1942

4. The American aircraft-carrier *Saratoga*—5. British aircraft-carrier *Ark Royal*

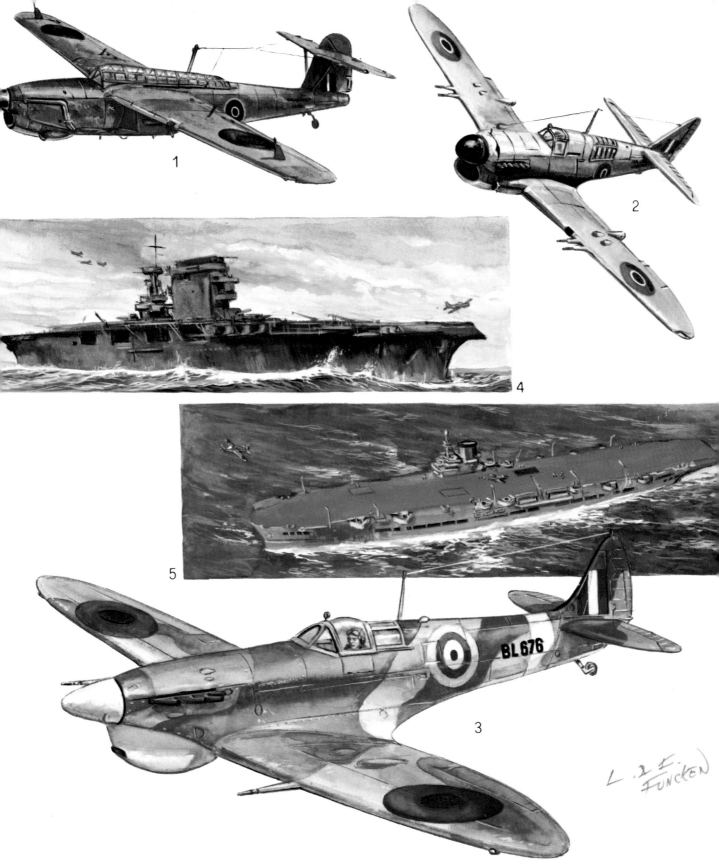

1

2

4

5

3

BL 676

L. & F.
FUNCKEN

The Japanese naval airforce was the first in the world to have planes which were not weighed down with all the technical paraphernalia resulting from dyed-in-the-wool traditionalism rather than practical observation.

Seaborne Japanese planes could serve just as well from land bases. They had been designed to do this without affecting their ability to perform their main function. For this reason, they were superior to all the enemy's naval planes and better too than America's land-based fighters in 1941. And so the Japanese had an easy time to begin with.

It did not take the British and Americans long to borrow the idea and change it around by adapting their new land-based fighter planes (which were far more powerful and better armed) to fly from aircraft carriers.

THE GREAT NAVAL PLANES

Affectionately nicknamed 'The String Bag' by its pilots, the Fairey Swordfish biplane was an anachronism compared with RAF planes, and antiquated compared with even the oldest of its counterparts. But it did remarkably well, taking off quite unconcernedly, even in the most appalling weather.[1] Eventually capable of being turned into a seaplane on floats, the Swordfish looked a little like the German Arado and Heinkel series, or the Italian *aero-silurante* (Water Torpedo Boat).

The US navy was the first to experiment with dive-bombing, and ever since 1919 had considered this technique the ideal solution and far more efficient than coming in on the level to drop torpedoes as other planes did. Of the dive-bombers made in the United States, the most famous was the Douglas SBD (S for Scouting, B for Bombing, D for Douglas) Dauntless, which held the record for tonnage sunk and fewest losses. The most famous of carrier-based fighters was the Grumman F6F (F for Fighting, 6 for the model, and F for Grumman[2]) Hellcat. The most unusual without

1 See volume 3 of this series, page 72.
2 F for Grumman? as with L for Bell, O for Lockhead, Q for Bristol, T for Northrop, Y for Consolidated-Vultee, although D for Douglas and G for Goodyear.

doubt was the Sea Hurricane, an adaptation of the Hurricane nicknamed Hurricat, which from 1941 to 1943 was flown from some cargo ships in Baltic convoys, launched by CAM (Catapult Aircraft Merchantmen) catapults. Once the pilots had accomplished their mission and were out of fuel, they had to land on the sea and wait to be picked up before their planes sank. These one-flight planes are indeed worth a passing mention.

The Japanese Navy

As an island nation, Japan needed an extremely powerful navy to carry out its policy of expansion. Japan's first navy set sail towards Korea in 33 B.C., but it was not until the mid-19th century that the Japanese navy acquired European-style ships. They were bought in Holland at first, and then, in 1861, in Great Britain. A Frenchman, Émile Bertin, was adviser to the Japanese admiralty, and can be considered the father of the Japanese navy. But there is no doubt that it was largely an English fleet that sailed under the new flag of the Rising Sun – as English as the structuring of its crew. In 1894 this fleet crushed the Chinese with ease and, as if to prove that that was no flash in the pan, inflicted a catastrophic defeat on the Russian navy at Tsushima in 1905.

AMERICAN NAVAL AVIATION

1. Douglas TBD 'Devastator'. At the beginning of the war it was the US Navy's main torpedo plane, and inflicted heavy losses on Japanese merchant navy, but had heavy losses itself—2. Douglas SBD Dauntless (1941–1945). The US Navy's main light bomber which, although outdated, rendered good service in the Pacific. It was so extraordinarily tough that it suffered the fewest losses of all US Navy planes—3. Curtiss SBC Cleveland. It flew from the carrier *Hornet* in 1941.—4. Grumman F4F-3 Wildcat, the standard fighter at the beginning of the war—5. Chance Vought F4U-1 Corsair, the most powerful naval fighter of its time. The Japanese nicknamed it 'Whispering Death'

Batman's signals to planes landing on a carrier: 6. 'Lower your hook'—7. 'Nose down'—8. 'Nose up'—9. 'Go left'—10. 'Like this'—11. 'Cut motors'

The commander of the fleet at the time was Heihachiro Togo (1847–1934), who had been trained in the Royal Navy and, it seems, was a great admirer of Nelson.

From 1912 on ships were no longer bought from abroad, but were made at home. From 1914 the Japanese were making so many ships and such good ones that France bought twelve torpedo boats from Japan.

In the period between the two World Wars, Japan could not tolerate the Washington naval treaty's restrictions, which attempted to keep its fleet below the strength of the Anglo-American navy. Ignoring the treaty, Japan began building a navy whose size was commensurate with her political ambitions, so that by 1940, her fleet was made up as follows:

Ships of the line	18	
Heavy cruisers	12	
Light cruisers	28	
Aircraft carriers	9	(with about 300 planes)
Plane transporters	5	(with about 60 seaplanes)
Destroyers	131	
Submarines	70	(of all kinds)

It should be noted that in the Battle of Midway just three of the above-mentioned aircraft carriers accounted for 387 planes.

During the war, the Japanese navy grew by a million tons as follows: 1 battleship, 16 aircraft carriers, 60 torpedo boats and 130 submarines. By the end of the war, the majority of the admirals had died and the larger part of their magnificent fleet had been sunk.

However warlike they were, there is a poetry inherent in Japanese life. This can be seen in the naming of their ships: torpedo boats and light destroyers were always named after trees, flowers, fruits or birds; ships of the line after provinces and mountains; while aircraft carriers were named after birds or dragons, and heavy destroyers after different kinds of weather.

The Russian Navy

Until its reorganisation by decree on 30 December 1937, the Soviet fleet was made up only of old ships that had been acquired during the Revolution from the old Russian Imperial fleet.

The rebirth of a purely Russian navy began with the first five-year plan, apart, that is, from two patrol boats and a light cruiser built in Italy in 1934 and 1939 respectively. Beautifully elegant ships like the 'Kirov'-type cruisers began to appear alongside refurbished and updated older ships; but the USSR concentrated on light destroyers, escort torpedo boats and submarines. There was a big submarine fleet, with three categories: the first, oceanic, had submarines of more than 900 tons; the second had medium, and the third of low tonnage. Numerically it was the largest fleet in the world, with only a negligible percentage of older models kept for training.

JAPANESE NAVY

1. Officer in winter service dress. In summer the same uniform was in white, including shoes—2. Officer in full-dress uniform. Right: detail of cap badge. For NCOs the badge consisted only of a gilt anchor on a navy-blue oval ground—3. Sailor in fatigue dress—4. 1st officer in service dress. In summer the uniform was all white, including the top of the hat—5. Sailor in normal summer dress—6. Officer with field service dress cap—7. Naval parachutist. Apart from the anchor on the helmet, the army uniform was identical—8. Sailor in landing uniform—9. Pilot in summer dress—10. Pilot in winter dress

Ranks: 11. Admiral—12. Vice-Admiral—13. Rear Admiral—14. Captain—15. Commander—16. Lieutenant-Commander—17. Lieutenant—18. Ensign 1st class—19. Ensign 2nd class—20. Chief petty officer. Badges of rank worn on the arm: 21. 1st officer—22. Chief petty officer—23. 2nd class petty officer—24. 1st class Quartermaster—25. Quartermaster—26. Sailor 1st class—27. Sailor 2nd class

28. Armoured cruiser *Nagato*—29. Aircraft-carrier *Syokaku*—30. Cruiser *Atago*—31. Mitsubishi F1M2 (Pete), reconnaissance plane and light bomber also used as a fighter—32. Aichi E13A (Jake), the chief reconnaissance plane in the Pacific war—33. Aichi E16A 'Zuiun' – Wind of Good Omen (Paul), reconnaissance plane also used as a dive-bomber—34. Kawanishi 'Kyofu' – Powerful Wind (Rex), an excellent fighter but only built in small quantities. The names in brackets are the code names used by the Americans

1   2   3   4   5   6   7   8

21   22

11   12   13   14   15   25

23   24   16   17   18   19   20   26   27

31   32

28

33

29

9   10   34   30

The naval high command had commissioned a large number of torpedo launches and fast patrol boats. Russia has thousands of miles of coastland and it was strategically vital to keep the great river estuaries free. On the other hand, Russia was not so well equipped in naval aviation, and before war broke out had only one aircraft carrier with just twenty-two planes on board. Called the *Stalin*, it was stationed in the Black Sea.

Owing to its geographical situation, Soviet Russia had had to set up its naval bases in many different seas. But it should be noted that there was a network of canals joining the Volga to the Dvina and to the Don, so that some smaller ships could pass from Archangel to Astrakhan and on to Sebastopol.

The Russian navy was divided into four fleets: the Baltic fleet, the Black Sea fleet, the Arctic Ocean fleet, and the Pacific fleet, with four small fleets on the Caspian sea, the Volga, Lake Onega and Lake Amur (between Siberia and China). Sailors wore initials representing the fleet or flotilla they belonged to on their epaulettes. At the onset of hostilities, the Soviet navy was made up as follows:

Ships of the line	3 (2)
Cruisers	5 (4)
Torpedo destroyers	24 (22)
Torpedo boats	17
Escort destroyers	30 (?)
Ocean-going submarines	40 (?)
Medium submarines	80 (?)
Light submarines	60 (?)

NB: Figures in brackets represent vessels under construction.

Besides this, the fleet had a number of dredging sloops, submarine-chasers, high-speed launches, gunboats for patrolling and river hydroplanes, and a powerful fleet of icebreakers which tried to keep the lines of communication to the Far East open via the Northern passage.

Although it never took part in a major sea battle, the Soviet fleet suffered some serious losses during its support operations at Leningrad and Sebastopol or while protecting convoys of supplies sent by the Allies. In 1942 the Russians had lost about 130 ships including two ships of the line and four cruisers.

So we come to the end of the four volumes which describe the appearance of the many men and women who took part in this the greatest drama in human history. Although some readers will be too young to have had first-hand experience of those dark days, it would be a mistake to see these books as no more than a catalogue of uniforms and weapons of a bygone age. It is to be hoped that all our careful documentation in no way conceals the agony and suffering which are an inevitable part of all military triumphs.

RUSSIAN NAVY

1. Officer in service dress—2. Officer in full-dress uniform—3. Officer in summer dress—4. Officer in winter dress—5 and 6. NCOs in anorak and jacket. Detail of cap badge—7. Gunner in winter battledress. This same short coat was used in winter by NCOs and sailors with their respective headgear (see figs 5, 6 and 8)—8 and 9. Sailors in summer and winter uniform

Ranks: 10. Admiral of the Fleet—11. Admiral—12. Vice-Admiral—13. Rear Admiral—14. Commodore—15. Captain—16. Commander—17. Lieutenant-Commander—18. Lieutenant—19. Ensign 1st class—20. Ensign 2nd class. Political commissars wore red stars and gold braiding on a red cloth ground on their shoulders. Mechanics and engineers had gold stars and braiding, with dark blue as the distinctive colour on their shoulders. Officers in the naval air force differed from the above by having a characteristic light-blue colour. Commissariat officers, doctors and officers of coastal defence had silver stars and braiding with, as colour identification, black, green and dark brown respectively—21. 1st officer—22. Chief petty officer in the Black Sea fleet—23. Petty officer 1st class (Baltic)—24. Petty officer 2nd class (Pacific)—25. 2nd officer (Arctic)—26. Sailor in the Caspian fleet—27. Officer's cap badge—28. Visor for senior officer's (up to the rank of Rear Admiral)—29. Captain's visor

30. Ship of the line *Marat*—31. Cruiser *Krasni-Kavkaz*—32. Cruiser *Profintern*—33. Beriev BE-2 (1931)—34. Chetverikov MDR-6 (1939). In spite of their age, these planes, particularly the Beriev, made themselves useful throughout the war in a variety of duties

PRINCIPAL WORKS CONSULTED

Les uniformes de l'armée française, Cdt E. L. Bucquoy and M. Toussaint

L'Armée française 1939–1940, A. Dépréaux

L'Armée française, M. Toussaint

Soldats d'hier et d'aujourd'hui, M. Toussaint

Uniformes de l'armée française, 1937, L'Uniforme Officiel

L'Armée française, H. de Foucauld

L'Armée française, Handbook of the Belgian army

Uniformen der Deutschen Wehrmacht, Eberhard Kettler

Die Soldaten Europas, Knötel and Jantke

Der Deutsche Soldatenkalender

Deutsches Soldatenjarhbuch

Die Deutsche Wehrmacht, 1935–45, Dr Klietmann

Souvenirs d'un soldat, H. Guderian

Alerte, parachutistes! A. von Hove

Kreta, Sieg der Kühnsten, F. A. Dahm and H. G. Schnitzer

Das Reichsheer und seine Tradition, Album of cigarette cards

Handbuch der Uniformkunde, R. Knötel and Sieg

Organisationsbuch der NSDAP, 1940

Le rôle de l'armée belge en 1940, General Baron Verhaegen

La Campagne des 18 jours et la reddition de l'armée belge, Saint-Yves

Dix-huit jours entre l'enclume et le marteau, H. Anrys

L'Armée soviétique de 1917 à 1957

Die Entwicklung der Taktik der Sowjetarmee im Grossen Vaterländischen Krieg, General Frunze

Suomen Puolustusvoimat

Zotnierz Polski, K. Linder, H. Wiewiora and T. Woznicki

Small Arms of the World, Smith and Smith

Kampfpanzer 1916–1966, Von Senger and Etterlin

Die Deutschen Panzer, Von Senger and Etterlin

German Tanks, B. T. White

British Tanks, B. T. White

Tanks, A. Halle and C. Demand

Corazatti Italiani, R. Pafi, C. Falessi and G. Fiore

Tanks, Macksley and Batchelor

Great Weapons of World War II, J. Kirk and R. Young

Aircraft Camouflage and Markings, B. Robertson

Famous Fighters, W. Green

Fighters, W. Green (4 vols)

Magazines: *Signal, Der Adler, Cadran, Marine nationale*

Bulletins: *La Figurine* (Belgium), *Passepoil* (La Société française des collectionneurs de figurines historiques), *La Sabretache* (France)